Appalachian
North Carolina Georgia

Appalachian Trail Guide to North Carolina-Georgia

Davenport Gap, North Carolina, to
Springer Mountain, Georgia,
including
the Great Smoky Mountains National Park

and side trails

Jack Coriell
Alan Duff
Dick Ketelle
Nancy Shofner

Field Editors

Eleventh Edition

Appalachian Trail Conference
Harpers Ferry

Cover photo: Stover Creek, Georgia
© 1998, Dwight Brown

© 1998, The Appalachian Trail Conference
P.O. Box 807
Harpers Ferry, West Virginia 25425

ISBN 1-889386-06-5

Eleventh Edition
Printed in the United States of America on recycled paper.

Preface

This eleventh edition of the *Appalachian Trail Guide to North Carolina-Georgia* contains detailed Trail data for the Appalachian Trail from Davenport Gap, at the northeastern end of the Great Smoky Mountains National Park, to Springer Mountain, Georgia, the southern terminus of the 14-state Appalachian Trail, and includes side trails in the Great Smokies, the Nantahalas, and Georgia.

This volume represents the cumulative work of many people over many years. It builds on the labors of committees and collectors of Trail data who provided material for four editions of the *Guide to the Appalachian Trail in the Southern Appalachians* and the previous ten editions of this guide. The editors especially would like to recognize, and express appreciation for, the many years of dedicated work of Lionel Edney of the Smoky Mountains Hiking Club, the Rev. A. Rufus Morgan of the Nantahala Hiking Club, and Henry Morris of the Georgia Appalachian Trail Club, Inc. (GATC). Those individuals, now all deceased, pioneered and supplied carefully prepared Trail data from their sections for many years. Although subsequent changes have been made, and new editors added, the work of those three still forms much of the material contained in this guide.

For this edition, Trail data have been supplied by the following individuals: Dick Ketelle supplied material for the Great Smokies; Alan Duff supplied material for the three northernmost sections of the Nantahala National Forest; Jack and Kay Coriell of the Nantahala Hiking Club researched and wrote the data for the Trail in the five southernmost sections of the Nantahala National Forest; and Nancy Shofner, Georgia Appalachian Trail Club, provided data for the Georgia section.

Constant changes occur along the Trail route. Those observing changes in approaches, accommodations, new trails, or anything that affects the data in the guide are requested to report such findings to the Publications Department, Appalachian Trail Conference, P.O. Box 807, Harpers Ferry, WV 25425, or call (304) 535-6331.

Contents

Notice To All Trail Users

The information contained in this publication is the result of the best effort of the publisher, using information available to it at the time of printing. Changes resulting from maintenance work and relocations are constantly occurring, and, therefore, no published route can be regarded as precisely accurate at the time you read this notice.

Notices of pending relocations are indicated in this guide. Maintenance of the Trail is conducted by volunteers in maintaining clubs listed in the guidebook, and questions about the exact route of the Trail should be addressed to the maintaining clubs or to the Appalachian Trail Conference, 799 Washington Street, P.O. Box 807, Harpers Ferry, WV 25425-0807; telephone, (304) 535-6331. On the Trail, please pay close attention to—and follow—the white blazes and any directional signs.

Responsibility for Safety

It is extremely important to plan your hike, especially in places where water is scarce. Purify water drawn from any source. Water purity cannot be guaranteed. The Appalachian Trail Conference and the various maintaining clubs attempt to locate good sources of water along the Trail but have no control over these sources and cannot, in any sense, be responsible for the quality of the water at any given time. You must determine the safety of all water you use.

Certain risks are inherent in any Appalachian Trail hike. Each A.T. user must accept personal responsibility for his or her safety while on the Trail. The Appalachian Trail Conference and its member maintaining clubs cannot ensure the safety of any hiker on the Trail, and, when undertaking a hike on the Trail, each user thereby assumes the risk for any accident, illness, or injury that might occur on the Trail.

Enjoy your hike, but please take all appropriate precautions for your safety and well-being.

Although criminal acts are probably less common on the Appalachian Trail than in most other human environments, they do occur. Crimes of violence, including murder and rape, have been committed over the years. It should be noted, however, that such serious crimes on the A.T. have a frequency rate on the order of fewer than one per year or less, on a trail that enjoys three to four million visitors in the same period. Even if such events are less common on the Trail than elsewhere, criminals can be more difficult to deal with because of the remoteness of most of the Trail. When hiking, you must assume the need for at least the same level of prudence as you would exercise if walking the streets of a strange city or an unknown neighborhood.

A few elementary suggestions can be noted. It is best not to hike alone, but do not assume safety just because you are hiking with a partner. Be cautious of strangers. Be sure that family and/or friends know your planned itinerary and timetable. If you customarily use a "Trail name," your home contacts should know what it is. Although telephones are rarely handy along the Trail, if you can reach one, dial 911 or ask the operator to connect you to the state police if you are the victim of, or a witness to, a crime.

The carrying of firearms is **not** recommended. The risks of accidental injury or death far outweigh any self-defense value that might result from arming oneself. In any case, guns are illegal on national parklands and in certain other jurisdictions as well.

Be prudent and cautious. Trust your gut.

How to Use This Guide

The Trail data in this guide have been divided into three major sections: The Smokies, southern North Carolina, and Georgia. The chapters for each Trail section are divided into three parts. The first part includes general information needed primarily for planning. This material is arranged under individual headings in the following order:

Brief Description of Section
Points of Interest
Road Approaches
Maps
Shelters and Campsites
Public Accommodations and Supplies

The detailed "Trail Description," the actual guide to the footpath, follows in two parts. Data are given first for walking south on the Trail and then for walking north. Trail data are presented in both directions of travel so hikers do not have to mentally reverse Trail descriptions. A column of distances on the left gives the mileage from the start of the section to important points along the Trail. Each point (such as stream crossings, shelters, summits, or important turns) is described briefly, followed by directions to the next point.

In each general section, a final chapter gives information on important side trails. If many side trails cross the A.T. in a certain area, no attempt has been made to describe them all. Rather, the reader is referred to other publications that describe trails in the area in more detail.

The Appalachian Trail

The Appalachian Trail (A.T.) is a continuous, marked footpath extending more than 2,160 miles from Katahdin, a granite monolith in the central Maine wilderness, south to Springer Mountain in Georgia, along the crest of the Appalachian mountains.

The Trail traverses mostly public land in 14 states. Virginia has the longest section, with 547 miles, while West Virginia has the shortest, almost 25 miles along the Virginia-West Virginia boundary and a short swing into Harpers Ferry at the Maryland border. The highest elevation along the Trail is 6,643 feet at Clingmans Dome in the Great Smoky Mountains. The Trail is only 124 feet above sea level near its crossing of the Hudson River in New York.

Trail History

Credit for establishing the Trail belongs to three leaders and countless volunteers. The first proposal for the Trail to appear in print was an article by regional planner Benton MacKaye (rhymes with sky) of Shirley, Massachusetts, entitled, "An Appalachian Trail, a Project in Regional Planning," in the October 1921 issue of the *Journal of the American Institute of Architects*. He envisioned a footpath along the Appalachian ridge line where urban people could retreat to nature.

MacKaye's challenge kindled considerable interest, but, at the time, most of the outdoor organizations that could participate in constructing such a trail were east of the Hudson River. Four existing trail systems could be incorporated into an A.T. The Appalachian Mountain Club (AMC) maintained an excellent series of trails in New England, but most ran north-south; the Trail could not cross New Hampshire until the chain of huts built and operated by the AMC permitted an east-west alignment. In Vermont, the southern 100 miles of the Long Trail, then being developed in the Green Mountains, were connected to the White Mountains by the trails of the Dartmouth Outing Club.

In 1923, a number of area hiking clubs that had formed the New York-New Jersey Trail Conference opened the first new section of the A.T., in the Harriman-Bear Mountain section of Palisades Interstate Park.

The Appalachian Trail Conference (ATC) was formed in 1925 to stimulate greater interest in MacKaye's idea and coordinate the clubs' work in choosing and building the route. The Conference remains a nonprofit educational organization of individuals and clubs of volunteers dedicated to maintaining, managing, and protecting the Appalachian Trail.

Although interest in the Trail spread to Pennsylvania and New England, little further work was done until 1926, when retired Judge Arthur Perkins of Hartford, Connecticut, began persuading groups to locate and cut the footpath through the wilderness. His enthusiasm provided the momentum that carried the Trail idea forward.

The southern states had few trails and even fewer clubs. The "skyline" route followed by the A.T. in the South was developed largely within the new national forests. A number of clubs were formed in various parts of the southern Appalachians to take responsibility for the Trail there.

Perkins interested Myron H. Avery in the Trail. Avery, chairman of the Conference from 1931 to 1952, enlisted the aid and coordinated the work of scores of volunteers who completed the Trail by August 14, 1937, when a Civilian Conservation Corps crew opened the last section (on the ridge between Spaulding and Sugarloaf mountains in Maine).

At the eighth meeting of the ATC, in June 1937, Conference member Edward B. Ballard successfully proposed a plan for an "Appalachian Trailway" that would set apart an area on each side of the Trail dedicated to the interests of those who travel on foot.

Steps taken to effect this long-range protection program culminated first in an October 15, 1938, agreement between the National Park Service and the U.S. Forest Service for the promotion of an Appalachian Trailway, through the relevant national parks and forests, extending one mile on each side of the Trail. Within this zone, no new parallel roads would be built or any other incompatible development allowed. Timber cutting would not be permitted within 200 feet of the Trail. Similar agreements, creating a zone one-quarter mile in width, were signed with most states through which the Trail passes.

After World War II, highway encroachments, housing developments, and summer resorts caused many relocations, and the problem of maintaining the Trail's wilderness character became more severe.

In 1968, Congress established a national system of trails and designated the Appalachian Trail and the incomplete Pacific Crest Trail as the initial scenic trails. The National Trails System Act directs the secretary of the interior, in consultation with the secretary of agriculture, to administer the Appalachian Trail primarily as a footpath and protect the Trail against incompatible activities and the use of motorized vehicles. Provision was also made for acquiring rights-of-way for the Trail, both inside and outside the boundaries of other federally administered areas.

In 1970, supplemental agreements under the act—among the National Park Service, the U.S. Forest Service, and the Appalachian Trail Conference—established the specific responsibilities of those organizations for initial mapping, selection of rights-of-way, relocations, maintenance, development, acquisition of land, and protection of a permanent Trail. Agreements also were signed between the Park Service and the various states, encouraging them to acquire and protect a right-of-way for the Trail outside federal land.

Slow progress of federal efforts and lack of initiative by some states led Congress to strengthen the National Trails System Act. President Jimmy Carter signed the amendment known as the Appalachian Trail Bill on March 21, 1978.

The new legislation emphasized the need for protecting the Trail, including acquiring a corridor, and authorized $90 million for that purpose. With 32 miles unprotected by mid-1998, this part of the project is expected to be completed by the end of this decade.

In 1984, the Interior Department delegated the responsibility for managing the A.T. corridor lands outside established parks and forests to the Appalachian Trail Conference. The Conference and its clubs retain primary responsibility for maintaining the footpath.

The Conference is governed by a volunteer Board of Managers, consisting of a chair, three vice chairs, a treasurer, a secretary, an assistant secretary, 18 regional members, and two at-large members.

The Conference membership consists of organizations that maintain the Trail or contribute to the Trail project and individuals. ATC membership provides a subscription to *Appalachian Trailway News*, published five times a year, and discounts of 15 to 20 percent on publications. The Conference also issues three newsletters: *The Register*, for Trail maintainers; *Trail Lands*, for contributors to its land-trust program, the Trust for Appalachian Trail Lands; and *Inside ATC*, for principal donors.

The Conference publishes books on constructing and maintaining hiking trails, official A.T. guides, general information on hiking and Trail use, and other Trail-related books. Annual membership dues range from $18 to $30, with life memberships available for $500 (individual) or $750 (couple).

Membership forms and a complete list of publications are available from the Appalachian Trail Conference, P.O. Box 807, Harpers Ferry, WV 25425; (304) 535-6331; (888) AT STORE (287-8673); or <www.atconf.org> on the Internet. The visitors center at ATC's central office (799 Washington Street) is open from nine a.m. to five p.m. (Eastern time), Monday through Friday, and nine to four on weekends from mid-May through the last Sunday in October.

Maintaining Clubs

Volunteers from three member clubs of the Appalachian Trail Conference maintain the Trail in North Carolina (south of Davenport Gap) and Georgia. The clubs, their areas of responsibility, and total mileages maintained are:

Smoky Mountains Hiking Club
Wesser, N.C., to Davenport Gap, Tenn./N.C., 100.4

Nantahala Hiking Club
Bly Gap to Wesser, N.C., 58.5

Georgia Appalachian Trail Club, Inc.
Springer Mountain, Ga., to Bly Gap, N.C., 75.6

General Information

Trail Marking

The Appalachian Trail is marked for travel in both directions. The marks are white-paint blazes about two inches wide and six inches high on trees, posts, and rocks. Occasionally, on open ledges, stone cairns identify the route. In some areas, diamond-shaped A.T. metal markers or other signs mark the Trail. Two blazes, one above the other, signal an obscure turn, a change in route, or a warning to check blazes carefully.

When the route is not obvious, normal marking procedure is to position the blazes so that anyone standing at one blaze will always be able to see the next. When the footway is unmistakable, blazes frequently are farther apart. If you have gone a quarter-mile without seeing a blaze, retrace your steps until you locate one, and then check to ensure that you did not miss a turn. Since the Trail is marked for both directions, a glance back may locate blazes for travel in the opposite direction.

Side trails from the A.T. to water, viewpoints, and shelters usually are blazed in blue paint. Intersecting trails not part of the A.T. system are blazed in a variety of colors.

At trail junctions or near important features, the Trail route is often marked by signs. Some list mileages and other information.

Trail Relocations

Always follow the marked Trail. If it differs from the guidebook's Trail description, it is because the Trail recently was relocated in the area, probably to avoid a hazard or undesirable feature or to remove it from private property. If you use the old Trail, you may be trespassing and generating ill-will toward the Trail community.

Information on Trail relocations between guidebook revisions often is available from the ATC information department. Every effort has been made in this guide to alert you to relocations that may occur. Do not follow new trails that are not blazed, because they may not be open to the public yet.

Water

Although the A.T. may have sources of clean, potable water, any water source can become polluted. Most water sources along the Trail are unprotected and consequently very susceptible to contamination. All water should be purified by boiling, chemical treatment, and/or filtering before using. Take particular care to protect the purity of all water sources. Never wash dishes, clothes, or hands in the water source. Make sure food and human wastes are buried well away from any water source.

Equipment

The basic equipment rule is, never carry more than you need. Some items should be with you on every hike: the *A.T. Data Book* and/or a guidebook and maps; canteen; flashlight, even on day trips; whistle; emergency food; tissues; matches and fire starter; multipurpose knife; compass; rain gear; proper shoes and socks; warm, dry, spare clothes; and a first-aid kit (see page 21).

Take the time to consult periodicals, books, employees of outfitter stores, and other hikers before choosing the equipment that is best for you.

Getting Lost

Stop, if you have walked more than a quarter-mile (1,320 feet or roughly five minutes of hiking) without noticing a blaze or other Trail indicator (see page 5). If you find no indication of the Trail, retrace your course until one appears. The cardinal mistake behind unfortunate experiences is insisting on continuing when the route seems obscure or dubious. Haste, even in a desire to reach camp before dark, only complicates the difficulty. When in doubt, remain where you are to avoid straying farther from the route.

Hiking long distances alone should be avoided. If undertaken, it requires extra precautions. A lone hiker who suffers a serious accident or illness might be risking death if he has not planned for the remote chance of isolation. Your destinations and estimated times of arrival should be known to someone who will initiate inquiries or a search if you do not appear when expected. On long trips, reporting your plans and progress every few days is a wise precaution.

A lone hiker who loses his way and chooses to bushwhack toward town runs considerable risks if an accident occurs. If he falls helpless away from a used trail, he might not be discovered for days or even weeks. Lone hikers are advised to stay on the Trail (or at least on a trail), even if it means spending an unplanned night in the woods in sight of a distant electric light. Your pack should always contain enough food and water to sustain you until daylight, when a careful retracing of your steps might lead you back to a safe route.

Distress Signals

An emergency call for distress consists of three short calls, audible or visible, repeated at regular intervals. A whistle is particularly good for audible signals. Visible signals may include, in daytime, light flashed with a mirror or smoke puffs; at night, a flashlight or three small bright fires.

Anyone recognizing such a signal should acknowledge with two responses—if possible, by the same method—then go to the distressed person and determine the nature of the emergency. Arrange for more aid, if necessary.

Most of the A.T. is used enough that, if you are injured, you can expect to be found. However, if an area is remote and the weather bad, fewer hikers will be on the Trail. In this case, it might be best to study the guide for the nearest place people are likely to be and attempt to move in that direction. If it is necessary to leave a heavy pack behind, be sure to take essentials, in case rescue is delayed. In bad weather, a night in the open without proper covering could be dangerous.

Wildlife

Several species of animals typical of this part of North Carolina and Georgia can be seen on the A.T. Hikers should avoid direct contact with all wild animals, due to the risk of rabies. Rabbits, squirrels, skunks, raccoons, opossums, chipmunks, mice, deer, and beaver have all been seen along the Trail.

Pests

Rattlesnakes and copperheads are found in North Carolina and Georgia. See page 19 for the recommended treatment of snakebites.

Ticks, chiggers, no-see-ums, mosquitoes, and other insects could also be encountered. Carry repellent.

Poison ivy, stinging nettle, and briars grow along many sections of the Trail. Long pants are recommended. Trailside plants grow rapidly in spring and summer, and, although volunteers try to keep the Trail cleared, some places may be filled by midsummer with dense growth, especially where gypsy moths have destroyed the overstory vegetation.

Parking

Park in designated areas. If you leave your car parked overnight unattended, you may be risking theft or vandalism. *Do not leave valuables in your car.* Please do not ask Trail neighbors for permission to park your car near their homes.

Hunting

Hunting is prohibited in many state parks and on National Park Service lands—whether acquired specifically for protection of the Appalachian Trail or as part of another unit of the national park system. However, most of the boundary lines that identify those lands have yet to be surveyed. It may be very difficult for hunters to know where they are on NPS Trail lands. Hunters who approach the A.T. from the side, and who do not know that they are on Trail lands, may also have no idea that the Trail is nearby. The Trail traverses several other types of landownership, including national forest lands and state gamelands, on which hunting is allowed as part of a multiple-use management plan (national forests) or specifically for game (state gamelands).

Some hunting areas are marked by permanent or temporary signs, but any sign is subject to vandalism and removal. The prudent hiker, especially in the fall, makes himself aware of local hunting seasons and wears blaze orange during them.

Trail Ethics

Treat the land with care to preserve the beauty of the Trail environment and ensure the Trail's integrity. Improper use can endanger the continuity of the Trail. Private landowners may order hikers off their property and close the route. Vandalism, camping and fires where prohibited, and other abuse can result in Trail closure. Please follow a few basic guidelines:

Do not cut, deface, or destroy trees, flowers, or any other natural or constructed feature.

Do not damage fences or leave gates open.

Do not litter. Carry out all trash. Do not bury it for animals or others to uncover.

Do not carry firearms.

Be careful with fire. Extinguish all burning material; a forest fire can start more easily than many realize.

In short: Take nothing but pictures, leave nothing but footprints, kill nothing but time.

Dogs are often a nuisance to other hikers and to property owners. Landowners complain of dogs running loose and soiling yards. The territorial instincts of dogs often result in fights with other dogs. Dogs also frighten some hikers and chase wildlife. If a pet cannot be controlled, it should be left at home; otherwise, it will generate ill-will toward the Appalachian Trail and its users. Dogs cannot be taken inside of the Great Smoky Mountains National Park. Also, many at-home pets' muscles, foot pads, and sleeping habits are not adaptable to the rigors of A.T. hiking.

Ask for water and seek directions and information from homes along the Trail only in an emergency. Some residents receive more hiker visitors than they enjoy. Respect the privacy of people living near the Trail.

Keep to the defined Trail. Cutting across switchbacks, particularly on graded trails, disfigures the Trail, complicates route-finding, and causes erosion. The savings in time or distance are minimal; the damage is great. In areas where log walkways, steps, or rock treadway indicate special trail construction, take pains to use them. Those have been installed to reduce trail-widening and erosion.

First Aid Along the Trail

By Robert Ohler, M.D., and the
Appalachian Trail Conference

Hikers encounter a wide variety of terrain and climatic conditions along the Appalachian Trail. Prepare for the possibility of injuries. Some of the more common Trail-related medical problems are briefly discussed below.

Preparation is key to a safe trip. If possible, every hiker should take the free courses in advanced first aid and cardiopulmonary-resuscitation (CPR) techniques offered in most communities by the American Red Cross.

Even without this training, you can be prepared for accidents. Emergency situations can develop. Analyses of serious accidents have shown that a substantial number originate at home, in the planning stage of the trip. Think about communications. Have you informed your relatives and friends about your expedition: locations, schedule, and time of return? Has all of your equipment been carefully checked? Considering the season and altitude, have you provided for water, food, and shelter?

While hiking, set your own comfortable pace. If you are injured or lost or a storm strikes, stop. Remember, your brain is your most important survival tool. Inattention can start a chain of events leading to disaster.

If an accident occurs, treat the injury first. If outside help is needed, at least one person should stay with the injured hiker. Two people should go for help and carry with them notes on the exact location of the accident, what has been done to aid the injured hiker, and what help is needed.

The injured will need encouragement, assurances of help, and confidence in your competence. Treat him gently. Keep him supine, warm, and quiet. Protect him from the weather with insulation below and above him. Examine him carefully, noting all possible injuries.

General Emergencies

Back or neck injuries: Immobilize the victim's entire body, where he lies. Protect head and neck from movement if the neck is injured, and treat as a fracture. Transportation must be on a rigid frame, such as a litter or a door. The spinal cord could be severed by inexpert handling. This type of injury must be handled by a large group of experienced personnel. Obtain outside help.

Bleeding: Stop the flow of blood by using a method appropriate to the amount and type of bleeding. Exerting pressure over the wound with the fingers, with or without a dressing, may be sufficient. Minor arterial bleeding can be controlled with local pressure and bandaging. Major arterial bleeding might require compressing an artery against a bone to stop the flow of blood. Elevate the arm or legs above the heart. To stop bleeding from an artery in the leg, place a hand in the groin, and press toward the inside of the leg. Stop arterial bleeding from an arm by placing a hand between the armpit and elbow and pressing toward the inside of the arm.

Apply a tourniquet only if you are unable to control severe bleeding by pressure and elevation. *Warning: This method should be used only when the limb will be lost anyway.* Once applied, a tourniquet should only be removed by medical personnel equipped to stop the bleeding by other means and to restore lost blood. The tourniquet should be located between the wound and the heart. If there is a traumatic amputation (loss of hand, leg, or foot), place the tourniquet two inches above the amputation.

Blisters: Good boot fit, without points of irritation or pressure, should be proven before a hike. Always keep feet dry while hiking. Prevent blisters by responding early to any discomfort. Place adhesive tape or moleskin over areas of developing redness or soreness. If irritation can be relieved, allow blister fluid to be reabsorbed. If a blister forms and continued irritation makes draining it necessary, wash the area with soap and water, and prick the edge of the blister with a needle that has been sterilized by the flame of a match. Bandage with a sterile gauze pad and moleskin.

Dislocation of a leg or arm joint is extremely painful. Do not try to put it back in place. Immobilize the entire limb with splints in the position it is found.

Exhaustion is caused by inadequate food consumption, dehydration and salt deficiency, overexertion, or all three. The victim may lose motivation, slow down, gasp for air, complain of weakness, dizziness, nausea, or headache. Treat by feeding, especially carbohydrates. Slowly replace lost water (normal fluid intake should be two to four quarts per day). Give salt dissolved in water (one teaspoon per cup). In the case of overexertion, rest is essential.

Fractures of legs, ankles, or arms must be splinted before moving the victim. After treating wounds, use any available material that will offer firm support, such as tree branches or boards. Pad each side of the arm or leg with soft material, supporting and immobilizing the joints above and below the injury. Bind the splints together with strips of cloth.

Shock should be expected after all injuries. It is a potentially fatal depression of bodily functions that is made more critical with improper handling, cold, fatigue, and anxiety. Relieve the pain as quickly as possible. Do not administer aspirin if severe bleeding is present; Ibuprofen or other nonaspirin pain relievers are safe to give.

Look for nausea, paleness, trembling, sweating, or thirst. Lay the hiker flat on his back, and raise his feet slightly, or position him, if he can be safely moved, so his head is down the slope. Protect him from the wind, and keep him as warm as possible. A campfire will help.

Sprains: Look or feel for soreness or swelling. Bandage, and treat as a fracture. Cool and raise the joint.

Wounds (except eye wounds) should be cleaned with soap and water. If possible, apply a clean dressing to protect the wound from further contamination.

Chilling and Freezing Emergencies

Every hiker should be familiar with the symptoms, treatment, and methods of preventing the common and sometimes fatal condition of *hypothermia*. Wind chill and/or body wetness, particularly aggravated by fatigue and hunger, can rapidly drain body heat to dangerously low levels. This often occurs at temperatures well above freezing. Shivering, lethargy, mental slowing, and confusion are early symptoms of hypothermia, which can begin without the victim's realizing it and, if untreated, can lead to death.

Wind Chill Chart

Actual Temperature (°F)

		50	40	30	20	10	0	-10	-20	-30	-40	-50
		Equivalent Temperature (°F)										
Wind Speed (mph)	0	50	40	30	20	10	0	-10	-20	-30	-40	-50
	5	48	37	27	16	6	-5	-15	-26	-36	-47	-57
	10	40	28	16	4	-9	-21	-33	-46	-58	-70	-83
	15	36	22	9	-5	-18	-36	-45	-58	-72	-85	-99
	20	32	18	4	-10	-25	-39	-53	-67	-82	-96	-110
	25	30	16	0	-15	-29	-44	-59	-74	-88	-104	-118
	30	28	13	-2	-18	-33	-48	-63	-79	-94	-109	-125
	35	27	11	-4	-20	-35	-49	-67	-82	-98	-113	-129
	40	26	10	-6	-21	-37	-53	-69	-85	-100	-116	-132

This chart illustrates the important relationship between wind and temperature.

Always keep dry, spare clothing and a water-repellent windbreaker in your pack, and wear a hat in chilling weather. Wet clothing loses much of its insulating value, although wet wool is warmer than other wet fabrics. Always, when in chilling conditions, suspect the onset of hypothermia.

To treat this potentially fatal condition, immediately seek shelter, and warm the entire body, preferably by placing it in a sleeping bag and administering warm liquids to the victim. The close proximity of another person's body heat may aid in warming.

A sign of *frostbite* is grayish or waxy, yellow-white spots on the skin. The frozen area will be numb. To thaw, warm the frozen part by direct contact with bare flesh. When first frozen, a cheek, nose, or chin often can be thawed by covering it with a hand taken from a warm glove. Superficially frostbitten hands sometimes can be thawed by placing them under armpits, on the stomach, or between the thighs. With a partner, feet can be treated similarly. Do not rub frozen flesh.

Frozen layers of deeper tissue beneath the skin are characterized by a solid, "woody" feeling and an inability to move the flesh over bony prominences. Tissue loss is minimized by rapid rewarming of the area in water slightly below 105 degrees Fahrenheit (measure accurately with a thermometer).

Thawing of a frozen foot should not be attempted until the patient has been evacuated to a place where rapid, controlled thawing can take place. Walking on a frozen foot is entirely possible and does not cause increased damage. Walking after thawing is impossible.

Never rewarm over a stove or fire. This "cooks" flesh and results in extensive loss of tissue.

Treatment of a deep freezing injury after rewarming must be done in a hospital.

Heat Emergencies

Exposure to extremely high temperatures, high humidity, and direct sunlight can cause health problems.

Heat cramps are usually caused by strenuous activity in high heat and humidity, when sweating depletes salt levels in blood and tissues. Symptoms are intermittent cramps in legs and the abdominal wall and painful spasms of muscles. Pupils of eyes may dilate with each spasm. The skin becomes cold and clammy. Treat with rest and salt dissolved in water (one teaspoon of salt per glass).

Heat exhaustion, caused by physical exercise during prolonged exposure to heat, is a breakdown of the body's heat-regulating system. The circulatory system is disrupted, reducing the supply of blood to vital organs such as the brain, heart, and lungs. The victim can have heat cramps and sweat heavily. His skin is moist and cold; his face flushed, then pale. His pulse can be unsteady and blood pressure low. He may vomit and be delirious. Place the victim in shade, flat on his back, with feet 8 to 12 inches higher than his head. Give him sips of salt water—half a glass every 15 minutes—for about an hour. Loosen his clothes. Apply cold cloths.

Heat stroke and *sun stroke* are caused by the failure of the heat-regulating system to cool the body by sweating. They are emergency, life-threatening conditions. Body temperature can rise to 106 degrees or higher. Symptoms include weakness, nausea, headache, heat cramps, exhaustion, body temperature rising rapidly, pounding pulse, and high blood pressure. The victim may be delirious or comatose. Sweating will stop before heat stroke becomes apparent. Armpits may be dry and skin flushed and pink, then turning ashen or purple in later stages. Move victim to a cool place immediately. Cool the body in any way possible (*e.g.*, sponging). Body temperature must be regulated artificially from outside the body until the heat-regulating system can be rebalanced. Be careful not to overchill once temperature goes below 102 degrees.

Heat weakness causes fatigue, headache, mental and physical inefficiency, heavy sweating, high pulse rate, and general weakness. Drink plenty of water, find as cool a spot as possible, keep quiet, and replenish salt loss.

Sunburn causes redness of the skin, discoloration, swelling, and pain. It occurs rapidly and can be severe at higher elevations. It can be prevented by applying a commercial sun screen; zinc oxide is the most effective. Protect from further exposure and cover the area with ointment and a dressing. Give the victim large amounts of fluids.

Artificial Respiration

Artificial respiration might be required when an obstruction constricts the air passages or after respiratory failure caused by air being depleted of oxygen, such as after electrocution, by drowning, or because of toxic gases in the air. Quick action is necessary if the victim's lips, fingernail beds, or tongue have become blue, if he is unconscious, or if the pupils of his eyes become enlarged.

If food or a foreign body is lodged in the air passage and coughing is ineffective, try to remove it with the fingers. If the foreign body is inaccessible, grasp the victim from behind, and with one hand hold the opposite wrist just below the breastbone. Squeeze rapidly and firmly, expelling air forcibly from the lungs to expel the foreign body. Repeat this maneuver two to three times, if necessary.

If breathing stops, administer artificial respiration, since air can be forced around the obstruction into the lungs. The mouth-to-mouth, or mouth-to-nose, method of forcing air into the victim's lungs should be used. The preferred method, protecting yourself with a mask or other cloth barrier, is:

1. Clear the victim's mouth of any obstructions.
2. Place one hand under the victim's neck, and lift.
3. Place heel of the other hand on the forehead, and tilt head backwards. (Maintain this position during procedure.) Use thumb and index finger to pinch nostrils.
4. Open your mouth, and make a seal with it over the victim's mouth. If the victim is a small child, cover both the nose and the mouth.
5. Breathe deeply, and blow out about every five seconds, or 12 breaths a minute.
6. Watch the victim's chest for expansion.
7. Listen for exhalation.

Poison Ivy

Poison ivy is the most common plant found along the Trail that irritates the skin. It is most often found as a vine trailing near the ground or climbing on fences or trees, sometimes up to 20 feet from the ground. A less common variety that is often unrecognized is an erect shrub, standing alone and unsupported, up to 10 feet tall.

The leaves are in clusters of three, the end leaf with a longer stalk and pointed tip, light green in spring but darkening as the weeks pass. The inconspicuous flowers are greenish; the berries, white or cream. The irritating oil is in all parts of the plant, even in dead plants, and is carried in the smoke of burning plants. Those who believe themselves immune may find that they are seriously susceptible if the concentration is great enough or the toxins are ingested.

If you have touched poison ivy, wash immediately with strong soap (but not with one containing added oil). If a rash develops in the next day or so, treat it with calamine lotion or Solarcaine. Do not scratch. If blisters become serious or the rash spreads to the eyes, see a doctor.

Lyme Disease

Lyme disease is contracted from bites of certain infected ticks. Hikers should be aware of the symptoms and monitor themselves and their partners for signs of the disease. When treated early, Lyme disease can usually be cured with antibiotics. (Its occurrence is greater along the northern mid-Atlantic areas of the Trail than in the sections covered by this guide.)

Inspect yourself for ticks and tick bites at the end of each day. The four types of ticks known to spread Lyme disease are smaller than the dog tick, about the size of a pin head, and not easily seen. They are often called "deer ticks" because they feed during one stage of their life cycle on deer, a host for the disease.

The early signs of a tick bite infected with Lyme disease are a red spot with a white center that enlarges and spreads, severe fatigue, chills, headaches, muscle aches, fever, malaise, and a stiff neck. However, one-quarter of all people with an infected tick-bite show none of the early symptoms.

Later effects of the disease, which may not appear for months or years, are severe fatigue, dizziness, shortness of breath, cardiac irregularities, memory and concentration problems, facial paralysis, meningitis, shooting pains in the arms and legs, and other symptoms resembling multiple sclerosis, brain tumors, stroke, alcoholism, depression, Alzheimer's disease, and *anorexia nervosa*.

It is not believed people can build a lasting immunity to Lyme disease, but vaccines are being worked on. A hiker who has contracted and been treated for the disease should still take precautions.

Hantavirus

The Trail community learned in the fall of 1994 that—18 months earlier—an A.T. thru-hiker had contracted a form of the deadly hantavirus about the same time the infection was in the news because of outbreaks in the Four Corners area of the Southwest. After a month-long hospitalization, he recovered fully and came back to the A.T. in 1995 to finish his hike.

Federal and state health authorities are still not certain but surmise that the hiker picked up the airborne virus somewhere in

Virginia. (The virus travels from an infected deer mouse, characterized by its white belly, through its evaporating urine, nesting materials, droppings, and saliva into the air.)

Hantavirus is extremely rare and difficult to "catch." Prevention measures are relatively simple: Air out a closed, mice-infested structure for an hour before occupying it; don't pitch tents or place sleeping bags in areas in proximity to rodent droppings or burrows or near areas that may shelter rodents or provide food for them. Don't sleep on the bare ground, use a mat or tent with a floor or ground cloth; in shelters, ensure that the sleeping surface is at least 12 inches above the ground. Don't handle or play with any mice that show up at the campsite, even if they appear friendly; treat your water; wash your hands if you think you have handled droppings.

Lightning Strikes

Although the odds of being struck by lightning are low, 200 to 400 people a year are killed by lightning in the United States. Respect the force of lightning, and seek appropriate shelter during a storm.

Do not start a hike if thunderstorms are likely. If caught in a storm, immediately find shelter. Large buildings are best; tents offer no protection. When indoors, stay away from windows, open doors, fireplaces, and large metal objects. Do not hold a potential lightning rod, such as a fishing pole. Avoid tall structures, such as flagpoles, fire towers, powerline towers, and the tallest trees or hilltops. If you cannot enter a building, take shelter in a stand of smaller trees. Avoid clearings. If caught in the open, crouch down, or roll into a ball. If you are in water, get out. Spread out groups, so that everyone is not struck by a single bolt.

If a person is struck by lightning or splashed by a charge hitting a nearby object, the victim will probably be thrown, perhaps a great distance. Clothes can be burned or torn. Metal objects (such as belt buckles) may be hot, and shoes blown off. The victim often has severe muscle contractions (which can cause breathing difficulties), confusion, and temporary blindness or deafness. In more severe cases, the victim may have feathered or sunburst patterns of burns over the skin or ruptured eardrums. He may lose consciousness or breathe irregularly. Occasionally, victims stop breathing and suffer cardiac arrest.

If someone is struck by lightning, perform artificial respiration (see pages 15 and 16) and CPR until emergency technicians arrive or you can transport the injured to a hospital. Lightning victims may be unable to breathe independently for 15 to 30 minutes but can recover quickly once they can breathe on their own. Do not give up early; a seemingly lifeless individual can be saved if you breathe for him promptly after the strike.

Assume that the victim was thrown a great distance; protect the spine, treat other injuries, then transport him to the hospital.

Snakebites

Reports of bites are extremely rare, but hikers on the Appalachian Trail may encounter copperheads and rattlesnakes on their journeys. These are pit vipers, characterized by triangular heads, vertical elliptical pupils, two or fewer hinged fangs on the front part of the jaw (fangs are replaced every six to 10 weeks), heat-sensory facial pits on the sides of the head, and a single row of scales on the underbelly by the tail. Rattlesnakes have rattles on the tail.

The best way to avoid being bitten by snakes is to avoid their known habitats and reaching into dark areas (use a walking stick to move suspicious objects). Wear protective clothing, especially on feet and lower legs. Do not hike alone or at night in snake territory; always have a flashlight and walking stick. If you see a snake, walk away; you can outdistance it in three steps. Do not handle snakes. A dead snake can bite and envenomate you with a reflex action for 20 to 60 minutes after its death.

Not all snakebites result in envenomation, even if the snake is poisonous. The signs of envenomation are one or more fang marks (in addition to rows of teeth marks), burning pain, and swelling at the bite (swelling usually begins within five to 10 minutes of envenomation and can become very severe). Lips, face, and scalp may tingle and become numb 30 to 60 minutes after the bite. (If those symptoms are immediate and the victim is frightened and excited, then they are most likely due to hyperventilation or shock.) Thirty to 90 minutes after the bite, the victim's eyes and mouth may twitch, and he may have a rubbery or metallic taste in his mouth. He may sweat, experience weakness, nausea, and vomiting, or faint one to two hours after the bite. Bruising at the bite usually begins within two to three hours, and large blood blisters may develop within six to 10 hours. The victim may have difficulty breathing, have bloody urine, vomit blood, and collapse six to 12 hours after the bite.

If someone you are with has been bitten by a snake, act quickly. The definitive treatment for snake-venom poisoning is the proper administration of antivenom.

Keep the victim calm. Increased activity can spread the venom and the illness. Retreat out of snake's striking range, but try to identify it. Check for signs of envenomation. Immediately transport the victim to the nearest hospital. If possible, splint the body part that was bitten, to avoid unnecessary motion. If a limb was bitten, keep it at a level below the heart. *Do not apply ice directly to the wound.* If it will take longer than two hours to reach medical help, and the bite is on an arm or leg, place a 2 x 2¼"-thick cloth pad over the bite and firmly wrap the limb (ideally, with an elastic wrap) directly over the bite and six inches on either side, taking care to check for adequate circulation to the fingers and toes. This wrap may slow the spread of venom.

Do not use a snakebite kit or attempt to remove the poison. This is the advice of Maynard H. Cox, founder and director of the Worldwide Poison Bite Information Center. He advises medical personnel on the treatment of snakebites. If you hike in fear of snakebites, carry his number, (904) 264-6512, and if you're bitten, give the number to the proper medical personnel. Your chances of being bitten by a poisonous snake are very, very slim. Do not kill the snake; in most Trail areas, it is a legally protected species.

First-Aid Kit

The following kit is suggested for those who have had no first-aid or other medical training. It weighs about a pound and occupies about a 3" x 6" x 9" space.

Eight 4" x 4" gauze pads
Four 3" x 4" gauze pads
Five 2" bandages
Ten 1" bandages
Six alcohol prep pads
Ten large butterfly closures
One triangular bandage (40")
Two 3" rolls of gauze
Twenty tablets of aspirin-free pain killer
One 15' roll of 2" adhesive tape
One 3" Ace bandage
Twenty salt tablets
One 3" x 4" moleskin
Three safety pins
One small scissors
One tweezers
Personal medications

The Appalachian Trail in
Southern North Carolina and Georgia

The southern Appalachian Mountains are the highest—and considered by some the most rugged—of the Appalachian chain. Much of the Trail route is ridgecrest travel above 5,000 feet in elevation.

With increasing elevation, particularly in the Great Smokies, the flora become similar to those found farther north. Southern Appalachian balds, great unforested summits comparable to the glaciated heights of New England, provide magnificent views.

Apart from the endless ridges, perhaps the most impressive feature of the southern Appalachians is the profusion of flowering shrubs, especially rhododendron, azalea, and laurel. In full bloom, their dense masses and "thickets" make the hiker's path one of great beauty. The floral display starts in mid-April and reaches its height in late June and July. Elevation influences the blooming season, and the blossoms occur much later on the summits than in the valleys.

The hiker will encounter a variety of trees here. The Great Smoky Mountains National Park contains more species than Europe. *The Appalachians*, a book by Maurice Brooks (Houghton Mifflin Co., Boston, 1965), vividly describes the Trail and its environment.

Most of the Trail route in this section is publicly owned, crossing the Great Smoky Mountains National Park and the Nantahala and Chattahoochee national forests. Public ownership provides protection under the National Trails System Act and ensures the preservation of the primitive aspects of the Trail environment.

Within the national forests, much of the Trail is graded and avoids steep ascents and descents. It bypasses many summits that do not have views in the summertime. As a rule, this type of trail is easier to hike than one that closely follows the ridgecrest. The graded Trail built by the National Park Service (NPS) in the eastern Smokies from Davenport Gap to Clingmans Dome (39.2 miles) is wider, has easier grades, and is more obviously constructed than U.S. Forest Service (USFS) trails. Contrasting with the graded Trail in the eastern Smokies, most of the 27.8-mile stretch of Trail from

Clingmans Dome to Shuckstack Mountain above the Little Tennessee River has an unworked footway.

The Trail in the southern Appalachians is off-road travel except for short distances on country roads. It is constructed and intended for hiking, except in short parts of the Great Smokies where horses are permitted. Use of motorized vehicles is expressly prohibited on the A.T. under the National Trails System Act.

Trail Route

Arnold Guyot's 1863 manuscript, "Notes on the Geography of the Mountain District of Western North Carolina," revealed that the southern Appalachians east of the Tennessee Valley and Cumberland Mountains form an enormous oval, extending from southern Virginia to northern Georgia, connected by high parallel transverse ridges. The Appalachian Trail uses portions of both forks and a connecting ridge, the Nantahala Mountains. The section between the Big Pigeon and Little Tennessee rivers is what Arnold Guyot called the "master chain" of the southern Appalachians. All but a short distance of it is in the Great Smoky Mountains National Park. Its terrain is the highest, wildest, and most primitive of the Appalachian chain.

The Great Smokies section of the A.T. ends on the south at the Little Tennessee River (Fontana Dam). The southbound route then turns back toward the Blue Ridge, the eastern fork of the oval. Leaving the crest of the Great Smokies at Doe Knob, it crosses the Little Tennessee River at Fontana Dam and climbs to the summit of Yellow Creek Mountain. The route then leads east.

The Yellow Creek-Wauchecha-Cheoah Range is a difficult section. At the Nantahala River, the A.T. turns south and joins a Forest Service trail for 58.7 miles. The Nantahalas are a land of 5,000-feet peaks and 4,000-feet gaps through an unbroken expanse of mountain ranges. In addition to Wesser, Wayah, and Siler balds, Standing Indian, the "Grandstand of the Southern Appalachians," is the dominating feature of this area. The 21.3-mile walk from Wallace Gap to Deep Gap over Standing Indian has few equals on the A.T. for scenic beauty.

The 75.6 miles in the Chattahoochee National Forest in northern Georgia are at a high elevation and are rugged. On Blood Mountain, the Trail elevation is still more than 4,400 feet. The two forks of the oval of the southern Appalachians meet at Springer Mountain, the southern terminus of the Appalachian Trail.

Great Smoky Mountains National Park

Between Davenport Gap and the Little Tennessee River, the A.T. lies within the Great Smoky Mountains National Park. The park is in both Tennessee and North Carolina, and the Trail follows the ridgetops along the state line. Park district-ranger offices are in Bryson City, North Carolina, and Gatlinburg, Tennessee. The main park headquarters is in Gatlinburg.

National Forests

In North Carolina, the Trail covered by this guide lies mostly within the Nantahala National Forest. The supervisor's office is National Forests in North Carolina, 160A Zillicoa Street, P.O. Box 2750, Asheville, NC 28802, (828) 257-4200. In Georgia, the Trail is within the boundaries of the Chattahoochee National Forest. The supervisor's office is at 1755 Cleveland Highway, Gainesville, GA 30501, (770) 536-0541.

Maps of the Trail Route

Since 1953, the Tennessee Valley Authority (TVA) has carried out an extensive mapping program with the U.S. Geological Survey (USGS). The Trail route covered by this guide is mapped on contoured quadrangles in 7½-minute series (about 0.4 mile equals one inch). Each section of the guide lists the specific maps that cover that part of the Trail.

Quadrangles may be obtained from Earth Science Information Center–USGS, 507 National Center, Reston, VA 20192, or by calling (703) 648-6892 or (202) 208-4047. They may also be purchased through outfitters or book stores. An area map for each state showing all the quadrangles and listing other maps may be obtained from USGS at the address listed above.

The USFS and Chattahoochee National Forest publish the Chattahoochee National Forest Map. This map shows the Trail, road accesses, campgrounds, *etc.* and may be obtained from the forest supervisor's office, 1755 Cleveland Highway, NW, Gainesville, GA 30501. A similar map of the Nantahala National Forest is available from the USFS Asheville office, 160A Zillicoa Street, P.O. Box 2750, Asheville, N.C. 28802, (770) 536-0541. Maps specifically of the A.T. are included with this guide—one for the Chattahoochee National Forest, one for the Nantahala National Forest, and one for the Smokies.

Maintenance of the Trail

Although responsibility for national scenic trails, including the Appalachian Trail, is vested by the 1968 National Trails System Act in the U.S. departments of the interior and agriculture, the work of maintaining the Trail is done largely by volunteers. Volunteers who maintain sections of the A.T. covered by this guide are members of the Smoky Mountains Hiking Club, the Nantahala Hiking Club, and the Georgia Appalachian Trail Club. Volunteers cut weeds, saw blowdowns, install water bars, and repair shelters. Trail maintenance is often done by club members on official club outings. In other cases, short sections of the A.T. are assigned to club members for individual maintenance. Some clubs call those members "section overseers" or "section maintainers."

Shelters

A continuous chain of shelters is spaced two to 13 miles apart throughout this section of the A.T. Each section of this guide lists shelters in the introductory information, and the distance to the shelter from the start of the section is given in the Trail description.

Most of the shelters in this section of the A.T. were built after 1937 by the NPS or the USFS, but a handful have been constructed in recent years by maintaining-club volunteers, sometimes with the help of an ATC volunteer crew.

Shelters are three-sided and have open fronts. They may be fitted with bunks or have a wooden floor that serves as a sleeping platform. Usually, a spring is nearby and sometimes a toilet, fireplace, tables, and benches. The hiker should bring cooking utensils and a small stove.

Those structures are called by different names in different areas: "lean-tos," "shelters" or "shelter cabins," and "Trail shelters." This guide uses the word "shelter" when referring to most of those structures.

Those facilities are provided primarily for the long-distance hiker who may have no other means of shelter. Persons planning short overnight hikes, who may have access to and from the Trail from road crossings, are asked to consider this and carry tents. This is a good practice anyway, since the Trail is heavily used and shelters are usually crowded during the summer months. Camps and other organizations are asked to keep their groups small (six to eight people, plus leaders). They should carry tents and not monopolize shelters. Although a shelter is available on a "first-come, first-served" basis, everyone is asked to cooperate and consider the needs of others who may have planned to use the shelter.

Group Hikes and Special Events

Special events, group hikes, or other group activities that could degrade the Appalachian Trail's natural or cultural resources or social values are to be avoided. Examples of such activities include publicized spectator events, commercial or competitive activities, and programs involving large groups.

The policy of the Appalachian Trail Conference is that groups planning to spend one or more nights on the Trail should not exceed 10 people and day-use groups should not exceed 25 people, unless the local maintaining organization has made special arrangements to both accommodate the group and protect Trail values. Some wilderness areas within national forests have lower limits that must be observed.

Compass Deviation

The compass deviation in this section is small (about one degree) and westerly. To change the compass course to the true geographical course, the amount of variation is applied to the left; that is, subtracted. In determining the compass course from the true geographical course, the deviation is applied to the right; that is, added.

Weather and Clothing

Be prepared for heavy, prolonged rainstorms in the South. Rain gear (full-length poncho, cagoule, or rain suit), a waterproof tent, waterproof matches, a change of clothing, and small cooking stove are essential.

Face, shoulders, and legs should be protected from sunburn. Shorts should be worn with caution.

On the balds, it may be cold, rainy, and windy at any time of the year. Be well-prepared with warm clothing, sleeping gear, and tents.

Some of this section is at elevations of more than 5,000 feet, which can mean winter conditions similar to sections much farther north.

Wind will reduce the air temperature by one to two degrees Fahrenheit for each mile per hour of its speed. For example, a wind of 20 miles per hour at 30 degrees Fahrenheit will reduce the effective temperature on your skin to about four degrees Fahrenheit (see wind-chill chart, page 13).

Geology of the Appalachian Trail in North Carolina and Georgia

The geologic evolution of North America's eastern continental margin is complex, involving at least three periods in which mountains were raised by tectonic forces in the Earth's crust, culminating with the opening of the Atlantic Ocean and building of the Appalachian Mountains chain some 300 million years ago. During those mountain-building events, bedrock was exposed to intense pressure and heat, which altered rock texture and mineral composition in a process known as metamorphism. Bedrock that underlies the Blue Ridge Mountains of the southern Appalachians ranges in age from about 600 million to 1 billion years. The bedrock illustrates varying degrees of metamorphism, which is evidenced by the rock types present (slate, which forms from shale sediments; marble, which forms from limestones; quartzites, which form from sandstones; and gneiss, which can form from a variety of parent rock types) and the minerals present (mica, garnets, and staurolite in more highly metamorphic rocks). In general, the bedrock is older and more highly metamorphic along the Trail in Georgia and North Carolina south of the Nantahala River than in the Smokies. The following description of geology along the A.T. between Springer Mountain and the Big Pigeon River is excerpted from *Underfoot: A Geologic Guide to the Appalachian Trail*, by V. Collins Chew (1993, Appalachian Trail Conference).

Most of the Appalachian Trail in Georgia rises and falls along the peaks and gaps of the eastern ridge of the Blue Ridge. The ridgeline generally separates streams flowing west to the Mississippi River from those flowing south to the Gulf of Mexico or the Atlantic Ocean. The Trail passes over several of the higher mountains in the state. Distant views to the southeast from the A.T. in Georgia are of the Piedmont Plateau-farmland, woodland, and a few scattered mountains. To the northwest are views of mountains and valleys of the interior of the Blue Ridge and of vast, unbroken forests, which are unusual south of Maine.

The rocks beneath the Trail in Georgia are roughly uniform and coarsely crystalline. There is little obvious relationship between rock type and topography, since mountain and valley are underlain by similar rock.

The first gold rush in the United States was centered in Dahlonega, Georgia, 14 miles southeast of Springer Mountain, in the 1830s, and former gold mines and prospects are scattered throughout the area.

At 4,461 feet, Blood Mountain is the highest point of the Appalachian Trail in Georgia and the second-highest in the state. Massive gneiss makes up the summit area of Blood Mountain. After a stretch through North Carolina, the A.T. closely follows the North Carolina-Tennessee state line and traverses many complex landforms, some related to the nature of the underlying rocks. The Trail leaves the eastern ridge of the Blue Ridge near Carter Gap, turns north, and crosses the Nantahala and Little Tennessee rivers. Then, it climbs to the west ridge of the Blue Ridge at the crest of the Great Smoky Mountains and the Tennessee state line.

Ten miles north of the Georgia line, the northbound A.T. hiker climbs above 5,000 feet for the first time at Standing Indian Mountain (5,498 feet). In this part of North Carolina, as along the Trail in Georgia, the topography has no obvious relation to the underlying rocks. Those rocks are coarsely crystalline and, in many places, show bands of light and dark minerals. The light minerals are generally quartz and feldspar; the dark minerals, micas and hornblende.

Just past Carter Gap, the Trail leaves the Blue Ridge Divide and follows the ridge that separates streams flowing into the Nantahala River and those flowing more directly to the Little Tennessee River. On this cross ridge, peaks above 5,000 feet are commonplace. Albert Mountain (5,250 feet) is particularly steep and impressive. A cliff at the top of Albert Mountain has vivid examples of the contorted bands of light and dark rock typical of coarse-grained gneiss. Farther north, Wayah Bald boasts three continuous miles of A.T. above 5,000 feet. Its rocks are stained a distinct orange by the weathered oxides of iron, which are not washed away by water. East of Wayah Bald is the Cowee Valley, near Franklin, North Carolina, where mines provide gravel for tourists to wash for rubies and a few semiprecious gems.

North of Wesser Bald along the A.T. are the first really significant changes in the rocks and topography. Slate, a fine-grained rock that breaks into sheets, is the first sign of change. Slate forms jaggy, craggy outcrops. The sparkling mineral mica, formed by the gentle heating of slate, is abundant in places.

A big event for the northbound hiker is the 2,700-foot descent to the Nantahala River, the first river crossing on the northbound A.T. and the lowest point so far along the Trail. The Nantahala River cuts its valley for about 10 miles along a belt of easily eroded rock. The belt is much longer than the Nantahala River Gorge and forms a low area west of the A.T. all the way from Springer Mountain. This band of rock, composed largely of marble and mica, is a bed of rock folded down into the older gneiss common in the area. The marble is slightly soluble in water and washes away. Erosion appears to have formed a long valley through the mountains, but, rather than being one stream valley, it includes several streams that cross or follow the lowland belt. The northbound hiker must climb out of the deep gorge and make the first 3,000-foot climb of the A.T. to reach Swim Bald and then a 700-foot climb to Cheoah Bald. The ridge just south of Cheoah Bald is a knife-edge outcrop of slate.

As the A.T. nears the crest of the Smokies, rocks along the way no longer show the shiny minerals seen to the south. They appear more like the sediments from which they were formed: slate from mud, siltstone from bedded silts, and sandstone from sand. Those sedimentary rocks underlie the A.T. throughout the Great Smoky Mountains National Park and almost to Max Patch Mountain. The Trail passes a type of rock found under the A.T. only in the western Smokies—a gray, massive rock called graywacke, containing pebbles of blue quartz, slate and the white mineral, feldspar, all in a fine-grained gray matrix.

From the main ridge of the Smokies, the view to the north reveals the much lower valley-and-ridge area beyond the outlying lower ridge of the Blue Ridge. Between Doe Knob and Thunderhead Mountain, the view of the first valley to the north reveals the open, low farmland area of Cades Cove, an isolated patch of the younger valley and ridge rock surrounded by Blue Ridge rock. Thunderhead Mountain provides expansive views of the area. Its summit is one of several grassy balds in the area that has probably existed this way since precolonial times.

Between Buckeye Gap and Silers Bald, the A.T. rises above 5,000 feet and remains at least that high for 34 miles, the longest length of the Trail above 5,000 feet.

Clingmans Dome (6,643 feet) was named for General Thomas L. Clingman, soldier, statesman, scientist, and explorer, who was the first to write about the Carolina mountains and the first to measure the dome's elevation.

Charlies Bunion shows the slate that makes much of the ridge in the Smokies. A severe fire following logging operations in 1925 allowed all the soil to erode, leaving the area bare. The Sawteeth, farther north on the A.T., are also made up of slate.

On its descent from the high country, the A.T. passes the trail to the spectacular, tilted rock ledges of Mt. Cammerer, then drops to 1,500 feet, and crosses the Big Pigeon River, where it cuts through the ridge in a deep gorge.

The following comment on the geological structure of the Great Smoky Mountains, which is exposed at Newfound Gap, is from *Nature Notes* (October 1939):

> *Motorists in the Great Smoky Mountains National Park who travel over the highway from Gatlinburg, Tennessee, to the Continental Divide, at Newfound Gap, and thence down to the village of Cherokee, North Carolina, may view one of the finest geological sections exposed in the entire East.*
>
> *Along this scenic drive, which mounts to over 5,000 feet above sea level, rock layers of slate, quartzite and conglomerate, tilted at astonishing angles, confirm the account given by geologists of how those very ancient mountains were brought forth. The Appalachians, which probably have been much higher in past eons than now, have been elevated and worn down not once but several times. Originally some of the strata laid down in prehistoric seas as muds and sands contained fossil. Those fossil-bearing rocks either have been worn away or so layered by heat and pressure that few evidences of the life that existed during their formation have been found up to the present time.*

Great Smoky Mountains National Park

Most of the 71 miles of the A.T. between the Pigeon River and the Little Tennessee River lie within the Great Smoky Mountains National Park, along the crest of the Great Smokies, the master range of the southern Appalachians. With the exception of the Black Mountains in North Carolina, the Smokies are the loftiest and most rugged mountains in the East. The trails within the park are maintained primarily by the National Park Service (NPS). The A.T. in the park is managed cooperatively by the Smoky Mountains Hiking Club, based in Knoxville, Tennessee, NPS, and ATC.

Although the first serious proposal to establish a national park in the Smoky Mountains was made before 1900, the efforts that were ultimately successful began in 1923. Private and public efforts to acquire land began in 1925. In 1928, John D. Rockefeller, Jr., contributed $5 million to match contributions of states and private citizens, and purchasing of land began in earnest. By 1930, 158,000 acres had been bought, and, by 1935, 400,000 acres. The park was formally dedicated in 1940 by President Franklin D. Roosevelt.

Additional information may be obtained from the park visitors center at Gatlinburg, Tennessee, and from the Smoky Mountains Hiking Club, P.O. Box 1454, Knoxville, TN 37938.

Maps

Trails Illustrated's Great Smoky Mountains National Park map, included with this guide, details topography, trails, shelters, and campsite locations, as well as other park facilities. Side-trail identification on this map is consistent with previous ATC maps and current guidebooks. For more detail, see the following quadrangles: USGS Waterville, Tennessee-North Carolina; Hartford, Tennessee-North Carolina; Luftee Knob, North Carolina-Tennessee; Mt. Guyot, Tennessee-North Carolina; LeConte, Tennessee-North Carolina; Clingmans Dome, North Carolina-Tennessee; Silers Bald, North Carolina-Tennessee; Thunderhead Mountain, North Carolina-Tennessee; Cades Cove, Tennessee-North Carolina; and Fontana Dam, North Carolina-Tennessee. Those maps are available from Earth

Sciences Information Center-USGS, 507 National Center, Reston, VA 20192, or by calling (703) 648-6892 or (202) 208-4047.

Campfires

Firewood is so scarce in the Smokies that hikers are advised to carry stoves. Stoves have the added advantage of providing cooking facilities in wet weather, which frequently occurs in the Smokies.

Water

A canteen, preferably two, is indispensable. Water sources are indicated in the Trail data. In dry seasons, it is often necessary at many of the springs to go farther down the mountain. Water also may be located on the slopes of other gaps, in addition to those specifically mentioned.

Bears

Bears are numerous at parking places and are attracted by food at shelters. Do not feed bears or leave food at shelters where bears can get it. Bears will steal food if it is not protected. Most shelters in the park have wire fencing across the open front. Some have separate food caches. If such storage places are not available, suspend food and packs from a rope or wire stretched high between two trees. Food left in automobiles may attract bears and result in damage to the car. Packs and tents may be similarly damaged. Excess food should be burned or carried out, not buried or left in the open. Tin cans and nonburnable refuse also should be carried out. Give bears a wide berth, particularly if they have cubs with them. It is dangerous to feed, tease, frighten, or molest them in any way.

Shelters

The park has a chain of 13 shelters along the A.T., five in the eastern part and eight in the western part. Those shelters were built especially by NPS for Trail use and are located at intervals of an easy day's travel. Use of each structure is limited to one night, and reservations are required. Users are expected to carry out all nonburnable refuse. Shelters in the park are listed in the introduction to each section. Fires are permissible only in the fireplace or at iron grills outside each shelter.

Camping Permits

Permits are required by NPS for use of the shelters along the A.T. This is not a requirement on most other parts of the Trail. It is a violation of Park Service regulations, punishable by up to a $500 fine, with possible jail sentence, for overnight hikers to travel in the Great Smoky Mountains National Park without a (free) camping permit. Hikers in the Great Smoky Mountains National Park may camp for only one night at a shelter—multiple-night stays are illegal. A.T. shelter permits for thru-hikers can be obtained at ranger stations and visitors centers in the park or at the USFS French Broad Ranger District Headquarters in Hot Springs, N.C., located across from the post office on the main street in town. Northbound thru-hikers may get permits at the TVA Fontana Dam Visitors Center. Advance reservations are required for others desiring shelter permits.

To prevent overcrowding at shelters and the deterioration of the Trail environment, the Park Service issues for a given night only as many camping permits as the capacity of the shelter. While other backpackers using backcountry shelters must make reservations; thru-hikers are exempt from this. Instead, the NPS automatically reserves three bunk spaces for A.T. thru-hikers at each shelter between April 1 and June 15. If there is no room in the shelter when thru-hikers with permits arrive, they must tent camp in the immediate vicinity of the shelter and store all food in provided food storage devices. Only thru-hikers are permitted to tent-camp at shelters. Hikers planning trips of more than one day should write to Great Smoky Mountains National Park, Gatlinburg, TN 37738, for regulations on shelter use and camping. Pets and firearms are not permitted on any park trails.

Trail Location

The original route of the A.T. extended the length of the Great Smokies to Deals Gap. Beyond, the Trail traversed 3.3 miles of privately owned land to Tapoco, where it crossed the Little Tennessee and Cheoah rivers on a highway bridge and then led back east along the crest of the Yellow Creek Mountains. This route was necessary because there was no other crossing of the Little Tennessee River.

The building of the TVA dam at Fontana on the Little Tennessee River made possible a Trail relocation that not only eliminated a difficult and circuitous route but added several unusual features to the Trail system: Fontana Dam, which serves as a crossing of the Little Tennessee; a 29-mile-long lake that forms the southern boundary of the Great Smokies; and Fontana Village, now a recreational center. At the suggestion of the Smoky Mountains Hiking Club, the Trail was relocated in 1946 and 1947 to leave the crest of the Smokies at Doe Knob, the point of most direct access to Fontana Dam.

From there, the route to Fontana Dam was constructed by NPS. Shuckstack, just off the route of the Trail, gives an outstanding view of the southern Appalachians. The relocation ascends from the dam to the original route on the crest of Yellow Creek Mountain near High Top. The relocations shortened the original route by 11.7 miles.

This change in route eliminated from the Trail two outstanding features, Gregory Bald and Parson Bald. Since the establishment of the park and the suspension of grazing, most balds have become overgrown, and their open features, which were their outstanding attraction, are disappearing rapidly. Gregory and Andrews balds are being kept open by cutting woody growth, however.

A portion of the original route has been officially designated as Gregory Bald Trail and continued as a side trail.

Fontana Dam and Fontana Village Resort

Fontana Dam, part of the TVA system, was constructed on the Little Tennessee River during World War II to furnish hydroelectric power. The dam is 480 feet high, the highest in the East and the sixth highest in the United States. The powerhouse and penstock are at the bottom, near the center of the river channel.

In May 1946, Fontana Village, which had been constructed at Welch Cove to house TVA construction workers, was leased to Government Services, Inc., for operation as a public recreation area. The village, now operated by Peppertree Resorts, Inc., is about four miles from the dam at an elevation of 1,800 feet, immediately at the base of the Yellow Creek Mountains. Extensive facilities are available, including a lodge, cafeteria, drug store, grocery store, post office, laundry, medical center, and about 300 houses.

Fontana Village Resort has an extensive recreation program. Hiking, fishing, horseback trips, and flower walks are featured.

The area is covered by the USGS Fontana Dam, North Carolina, quadrangle. Information on Fontana and a map may be obtained by writing Fontana Village Resort, Fontana Dam, NC 28733.

The dam, in creating the lake with a normal shoreline at an elevation of about 1,710 feet, flooded out N.C. 288 from Deals Gap to Bryson City. Hard-surfaced N.C. 28 leads from U.S. 129 to Fontana Dam (9.5 miles from Deals Gap) and continues to a junction with U.S. 19 nine miles south of Bryson City.

Davenport Gap (Tenn. 32-N.C. 284) to Newfound Gap (U.S. 441)
Section One
31.3 miles

Brief Description of Section

This section traverses the wildest, and at one time the most difficult, portion of the Great Smokies. From Davenport Gap (1,975 feet), it is a long, continuous climb of 3,025 feet over a distance of 5.2 miles to the crest of the state line, west of Mt. Cammerer, at the eastern end of the Great Smokies.

Beyond are many deep gaps and high peaks, with 11 major climbs and the same number of descents. After passing over Cosby Knob, the Trail descends to Camel Gap before ascending to Inadu Knob and Deer Creek Gap before it swings around Mt. Guyot a short distance from its 6,621-foot summit. The next peaks are Tricorner Knob, Mt. Chapman, Mt. Sequoyah, Pecks Corner, Porters Mountain, and Charlies Bunion. After passing Mt. Kephart, the Trail descends 955 feet to Newfound Gap. The route through the section is graded, with a grade of no more than 15 percent. The hiker passes a succession of panoramic views without having to pay constant attention to the footway.

The route is indicated by white-paint blazes as well as by dug footway. Board signs mark intersections with side trails.

Because much of the A.T. is on or near the state line, the slopes are designated in the Trail data as North Carolina or Tennessee.

Points of Interest

Much of the Trail in this section passes through remnants of the high-elevation spruce-fir forests. The spruce-fir forests of the Great Smokies are in a period of decline because of air pollutants and attack by the balsam wooly adelgid, a killer of mature fir trees. Overstory canopy trees have died, allowing sunlight to reach the understory, thus resulting in massive blackberry growth. At times, this growth nearly blocks the Trail.

Unlike the broader crest, south and west of Newfound Gap the crest is narrow, particularly in the section known as the Sawteeth, where one may stand astride the state line. The outstanding peaks are Mt. Kephart, named for Horace Kephart, an early A.T. planner, distinguished authority on the region, and author of *Our Southern Highlands*; the Jumpoff, which allows a magnificent northern view of the entire range as far as Mt. Guyot; Mt. Chapman, named in honor of Colonel David C. Chapman, who was instrumental in establishing the park; and Mt. Guyot, named for Arnold Guyot, whose explorations prior to the Civil War and manuscript map constitute valuable sources for a study of the region.

At the eastern end of the Great Smokies is Mt. Cammerer, formerly White Rock, renamed to commemorate the outstanding services to the Great Smoky Mountains National Park of early NPS Director Arnold B. Cammerer. The stone tower (5,025 feet) on Mt. Cammerer provides a 360-degree view of the Smokies. This is one of the most spectacular views along the Trail. Between Mt. Cammerer and Mt. Guyot is a section known as Hell Ridge, so named because of the devastation caused by forest fires on the North Carolina side and because it was difficult to travel.

The highest point in the section is about 6,360 feet, where the Trail swings around the Tennessee side of Mt. Guyot, a short distance below the 6,621-foot summit.

On clear days, views from Charlies Bunion are extraordinary. To the west are the Jumpoff and Mt. Kephart, to the northwest is Mt. LeConte, to the north are gorges on headwaters of Porters Creek, slightly northeast is Greenbrier Pinnacle, and to the east is the jagged knifelike section of the state line known as the Sawteeth Range. Charlies Bunion was formed in the 1920s when a cloudburst caused landslides on an area burned in a forest fire.

Road Approaches

From Davenport Gap north *via* Tenn. 32, it is 26.5 miles to Newport, from which, *via* I-40 or U.S. 70, it is 45.4 miles to Knoxville (71.9 miles from Davenport Gap); *via* Tenn. 32 and U.S. 321, it is 30.6 miles to Gatlinburg. South *via* N.C. 284 and 276, it is 29 miles to Dellwood, North Carolina, and U.S. 19, which leads to Asheville, 60 miles from Davenport Gap. A shorter route to Newport (19 miles north) and to Asheville (57 miles southeast) follows N.C. 284 to Mt.

Sterling Village (Big Creek Ranger Station and primitive campground a short distance upstream). There, turn left on the gravel
road beside Big Creek, and continue through Waterville and across
Browns Bridge to I-40. N.C. 284, while narrow and steep, has
extraordinary views of the eastern end of the park.

Public transportation is not available in Davenport Gap. Be-
cause of vandalism, it is not advisable to leave cars overnight near
Davenport Gap or leave valuables in your car. Park at the Big Creek
Ranger Station in seasons when rangers are present.

The southern end of the section is reached from U.S. 441, the
highway that crosses the Great Smoky Mountains at Newfound
Gap. From this highway, it is 16 miles to Gatlinburg and 55 miles to
Knoxville, both northwest in Tennessee, and 20 miles southeast to
Cherokee, North Carolina.

Maps

Refer to Trails Illustrated's Great Smoky Mountains National
Park map with this guide for route navigation. For additional area
detail, refer to USGS Clingmans Dome, North Carolina-Tennessee;
Mt. LeConte, Tennessee-North Carolina; Mt. Guyot, Tennessee-
North Carolina; Luftee Knob, North Carolina-Tennessee; Hartford,
Tennessee-North Carolina; and Waterville, Tennessee-North Caro-
lina, quadrangles.

Shelters, Campsites, and Water

This section has five shelters and 15 water sources. *Reservations
are required at all shelters.* The shelters are listed below:

Miles from Davenport Gap	Shelter
0.9	Davenport Gap
8.0	Cosby Knob
15.7	Tricorner Knob
20.9	Pecks Corner (0.4 mile from A.T.)
28.3	Icewater Spring

Public Accommodations and Supplies

Public accommodations and supplies are not available on or near the Trail at either end of this section. Stores, post offices, restaurants, and lodging are available at Newport, Cosby, Gatlinburg, and Cherokee.

Precautions

The many deep gaps and high peaks in this section involve considerably more climbing than a casual inspection of the route would indicate. Allow for extra time and exertion.

The section is easier to hike southwest to northeast, from Newfound Gap (5,045 feet) to Davenport Gap (1,975 feet), than in the reverse direction. In traversing the section from southwest to northeast, the climbing totals 4,608 feet and the downhill travel, 7,678 feet.

See information in the preceding chapter, "Great Smoky Mountains National Park," for advice about firewood, water sources and scarcity, wildlife protection, bears, and camping permits.

Trail Description, North to South

Miles	Data
0.0	From Davenport Gap (1,975 feet), at Tenn. 32 and N.C. 284, follow graded trail west, and cross small clearing.
0.2	Water can be found below and to left of Trail.
0.9	Reach **Davenport Gap Shelter**; accommodates 12; located 100 yards to right of Trail, with spring nearby. Ascend steadily.
1.9	Chestnut Branch Trail leads 2.0 miles to Big Creek Ranger Station and **campground.**
2.8	Reach lower Mt. Cammerer Trail, leading **7.8** miles to **Cosby Campground** on Tennessee side.
3.1	Reach side trail on left, leading 50 yards to spring.
3.2	Cross spur on North Carolina side, ascend, and skirt southern slope of Mt. Cammerer. Note spectacular Trail construction.

4.4 Pass through gap in spur off side of Mt. Cammerer, and ascend slope of mountain.

4.7 Reach small uphill site used as a camp by CCC in construction of Mt. Cammerer tower; just beyond is spring, on right.

5.2 Reach graded side trail on right leading 0.6 mile to Mt. Cammerer tower. Beyond side trail, route ascends.

5.4 Cross high point (about 5,000 feet), then cross spur on Tennessee side of Sunup Knob (5,050 feet), with good views.

6.7 Cross crest of Rocky Face Mountain, a spur on Tennessee side.

7.3 Descend to Low Gap (4,242 feet). Trails lead from here to Walnut Bottom (North Carolina side), following Low Gap Branch, and to **Cosby Campground** (Tennessee side), following Cosby Creek 2.5 miles. From Low Gap, climb 785 feet to Cosby Knob.

7.9 Water crosses Trail.

8.0 Reach **Cosby Knob Shelter**, 150 feet to left; accommodates 12; spring nearby. Trail enters Hell Ridge.

8.6 Cross spur on Tennessee side after swinging around North Carolina side of Cosby Knob (5,145 feet).

9.0 Cross spur, and pass around forested side of Ross Knob (5,025 feet) on Tennessee side.

9.5 Reach Camel Gap (4,645 feet). From here, Camel Gap Trail leads to Big Creek and Walnut Bottom. Ascend, swinging to Tennessee side.

10.5 Reach wooded side of Camel Hump Knob (5,250 feet).

11.9 Reach Snake Den Ridge Trail, which joins A.T. from Tennessee side. This trail goes by Maddron Bald and down Snake Den Mountain to **Cosby Campground**. Spring is about 0.8 mile down this trail. Follow A.T. around slope of Inadu Knob (5,941 feet). "Inadu" means "snake" in Cherokee and refers to snake dens on the mountainside.

12.2 Reach Yellow Creek Gap.

12.8 Reach Deer Creek Gap (6,020 feet). Fantastic views of Mt. Guyot, Luftee Knob, Balsam Corner, and Mt. Sterling can be seen from here.

13.3 Good view of English Mountain, Tennessee. Trail ascends.

13.4   Cross Pinnacle Lead, spur off Tennessee side of Old Black. Pinnacle Lead forms boundary between Sevier and Cocke counties of Tennessee.

13.6   Reach gap between Mt. Guyot and Old Black.

13.9   Pass Guyot Spring.

14.5   Cross Guyot Spur (6,360 feet), highest point on A.T. in eastern Smokies.

15.1   Reach sharp-ridged gap between Tricorner Knob and Mt. Guyot, then climb along Tennessee side of Tricorner Knob (6,100 feet). Balsam Mountain, leading from Tricorner Knob, forms boundary between Swain and Haywood counties of North Carolina. Tricorner Knob is junction of two major ranges, the Smoky and the Balsam, and was given its name by geographer Arnold Guyot.

15.5   Balsam Mountain Trail comes in on left. **Laurel Gap Shelter** is seven miles away *via* this trail; accommodates 14; spring nearby.

15.7   Come to trail junction. A.T. bears right. Left fork leads 100 yards to **Tricorner Knob Shelter** on North Carolina side; accommodates 12; spring nearby.

15.8   Reach Big Cove Gap (5,825 feet). Ascend, following state line between north and middle peaks of Mt. Chapman.

16.7   Reach high point of Trail on Mt. Chapman.

17.5   Reach Chapman Gap (5,650 feet).

18.2   Reach high point of Mt. Sequoyah (6,000 feet).

18.9   Cross Old Troublesome, a spur off Tennessee side of Mt. Sequoyah.

19.2   Reach Copper Gap (5,650 feet), then climb 250 feet to Eagle Rocks.

19.9   Water is located 800 feet down North Carolina side on northern end of Eagle Rocks.

20.0   Reach spectacular view of precipitous slopes and sharp gorges caused by headwaters of Eagle Rocks Prong.

20.4   Swing around western peak of Eagle Rocks (5,900 feet) and then around North Carolina side of Pecks Corner, junction of Hughes Ridge and state line.

20.9   Reach Hughes Ridge Trail on left. This trail leads to **Pecks Corner Shelter**, formerly Hughes Ridge; accommodates 12; spring nearby. To reach shelter, follow graded Hughes Ridge Trail south for 0.4 mile to gap, and then turn left, downhill, 100 yards in beech woods. About 100 feet beyond junction of Hughes Ridge Trail is intermittent spring on right side of A.T.

21.1   Cross Hughes Ridge.

22.2   Reach Bradleys View on state line, with unusually fine views into deep-cut gorge of Bradley Fork and over mountains in North Carolina.

23.5   Cross Woolly Tops Lead.

23.8   Pass around side of Laurel Top (5,865 feet).

24.8   Reach False Gap (5,400 feet). Good spring, located at former shelter site about 1/4 mile down northern slope. From False Gap, Trail ascends 100 feet to Porters Mountain.

25.5   Reach Porters Gap (5,500 feet), on state line, near junction of Porters Mountain and state-line ridge. Trail proceeds along crest of jagged range known as the Sawteeth.

26.9   Come into 0.8-mile section that was swept by fire following timbering operations in 1925. Spectacular views.

27.1   Dry Sluice Gap Trail, formerly Richland Mountain Trail, comes in on left from **Smokemont Campground**, 8.5 miles distant. *Via* this trail and Grassy Branch Trail, it is 3.7 miles to **Kephart Shelter**; accommodates 14; creek water.

27.2   Reach Dry Sluice Gap (5,375 feet). Water may be found about 400 feet down North Carolina side.

27.4   Pass around higher peak of Charlies Bunion and then around right side of precipitous western (lower) peak of the Bunion. Lower or western peak is sometimes called Fodder Stack; higher peak is called Charlies Bunion.

28.2   Pass spring on right.

28.3   Reach **Icewater Spring Shelter** on the left; accommodates 12; spring water.

28.6   Boulevard Trail enters on right. On Boulevard Trail, it is 5.3 miles to **LeConte Lodge and Shelter.** Accommodations are available at lodge from late March to early November; shelter accommodates 12. About 100 yards from A.T., spur trail off Boulevard Trail leads 0.8 mile to Mt. Kephart (6,150 feet) and the Jumpoff (6,100 feet). The Jumpoff has spectacular views.

28.9   Reach elevation of about 6,000 feet, and begin gradual descent to Newfound Gap.

29.4   Fine views of Clingmans Dome (6,643 feet), highest point
        in park, on A.T. to southwest, and of Thomas Ridge and
        Oconaluftee River gorge, to south.

29.6   Reach junction with Sweat Heifer Creek Trail, which leads
        down Kephart Prong on North Carolina side. The name
        Sweat Heifer probably came from the driving of cattle up
        this steep trail to high, grassy pastures. **Kephart Shelter** is
        3.7 miles down this trail; accommodates 14; creek water.

31.3   Reach U.S. 441 in Newfound Gap (5,045 feet) at parking
        area.

Trail Description, South to North

Miles   **Data**

0.0   From crest of U.S. 441 at Newfound Gap (5,045 feet), at
        northeast corner of parking area, follow graded Trail
        northeast along North Carolina side. The hardwoods are
        mainly yellow birch. The conifers are red spruce and
        Fraser fir, locally called balsam. This section lies in Swain
        County, North Carolina.

1.7   Pass graded Sweat Heifer Creek Trail, leading down
        Kephart Prong. The name Sweat Heifer probably came
        from the driving of cattle up this steep trail to high, grassy
        pastures. On North Carolina side, **Kephart Shelter** is 3.7
        miles down this trail; accommodates 14; creek water.

1.9   Fine views to southwest of Clingmans Dome (6,643 feet),
        highest point in park and on A.T., and of Thomas Ridge
        and Oconaluftee River gorge to south.

2.4   On state line, begin descent from elevation of about 6,000
        feet.

2.7   At trail junction, take right fork. Left is Boulevard Trail.
        On Boulevard Trail, it is 5.3 miles to **LeConte Lodge and
        Shelter.** Lodge accommodations are available from late
        March to early November. Shelter accommodates 12. About
        100 yards from A.T., spur trail off Boulevard Trail leads 0.8
        mile to Mt. Kephart (6,150 feet) and the Jumpoff (6,100
        feet), with spectacular views. From junction with Boule-
        vard Trail, swing around North Carolina side of Mt.
        Kephart.

3.0   Reach **Icewater Spring Shelter;** accommodates 12; spring water.

3.6   Enter 0.8-mile section swept by fire after timbering operations in 1925. Spectacular views.

3.8   Pass around left side of precipitous western (lower) peak of Charlies Bunion.

3.9   Pass around higher peak of Charlies Bunion. Lower (western) peak is sometimes called Fodder Stack; higher (eastern) peak, Charlies Bunion.

4.1   Descend to Dry Sluice Gap (5,375 feet). Water may be found about 400 feet down North Carolina side.

4.2   Reach junction with Dry Sluice Gap Trail, formerly Richland Mountain Trail. Take left fork. Right leads 8.5 miles to **Smokemont Campground;** *via* this trail and Grassy Branch Trail, it is 3.7 miles to **Kephart Shelter;** accommodates 14; creek water.

5.8   Pass through Porters Gap (5,500 feet), near junction of Porters Mountain and state-line ridge.

5.9   Cross crest of Porters Mountain on Tennessee side.

6.1   Cross spur of ridge on Tennessee side, and continue descent.

6.5   After drop of 100 feet from Porters Mountain, reach False Gap (5,400 feet). A good spring is located about 1/4 mile from northern slope from False Gap at former shelter site. Ascend steeply for 0.3 mile and then more gradually.

7.5   Pass around side of Laurel Top (5,865 feet).

7.8   Cross Woolly Tops Lead. Descend again, after gaining 400 feet in elevation since leaving False Gap.

9.1   On state line is Bradleys View, with unusually fine views into deep-cut gorge of Bradley Fork and over mountains in North Carolina.

9.6   Start ascent around Pecks Corner. Reach junction of Hughes Ridge and state-line range. Behind are good views of Laurel Top and the Sawteeth Range, with Mt. LeConte visible through False Gap.

9.9   Cross unnamed ridge on North Carolina side.

10.2   Cross Hughes Ridge.

10.4   Proceed ahead at junction with graded Hughes Ridge Trail. Hughes Ridge Trail goes to **Pecks Corner Shelter,** formerly Hughes Ridge Shelter. Built-in bunks accommodate 12; spring nearby. To reach shelter, follow graded Hughes Ridge Trail south 0.4 mile to gap, and then turn left, downhill, 100 yards in beech woods. Beyond, Hughes Ridge Trail continues to **Smokemont Campground**.

10.6   Follow state line with good views of Eagle Rocks and Mounts Sequoyah, Chapman, and Guyot.

10.9   Swing to North Carolina side around western peak of Eagle Rocks (5,900 feet).

11.3   Reach spectacular view of precipitous Tennessee slope into sharp gorges carved out by headwaters of Eagle Rocks Prong. Trail has ascended 500 feet from gap just west of Pecks Corner and Hughes Ridge.

11.4   At northern end of Eagle Rocks, water can be found about 800 feet down North Carolina side.

12.1   Enter Copper Gap (5,650 feet).

12.4   Cross Old Troublesome, a spur off Tennessee side of Mt. Sequoyah.

13.1   Cross high point of Mt. Sequoyah (6,000 feet).

13.8   Reach Chapman Gap (5,650 feet). From Chapman Gap, follow North Carolina side.

14.6   Reach high point of Trail on Mt. Chapman, after climbing 600 feet from Chapman Gap.

15.5   Reach Big Cove Gap (5,825 feet). Ascend Tricorner Knob.

15.6   Reach trail junction. To follow A.T., bear left. Right leads 100 yards to **Tricorner Knob Shelter** on North Carolina side. Built-in bunks accommodate 12; spring nearby.

15.8   Reach junction with side trail. A.T. turns left. To right is graded Balsam Mountain Trail to Hyatt Ridge. **Laurel Gap Shelter** is seven miles *via* this trail; accommodates 14; spring nearby. Swing to Tennessee side, and climb around side of 6,100-foot Tricorner Knob. Tricorner Knob is at junction of two major ranges, the Smoky and the Balsam, and was given its name by geographer Arnold Guyot. Balsam Mountain, leading off from knob, forms boundary between Swain and Haywood counties of North Carolina.

16.2   Follow state line through sharp-ridged gap between Tricorner Knob and Mt. Guyot, with fine views into North Carolina, particularly of Mt. Sterling and North Carolina side of Hell Ridge. Follow Tennessee slope of Mt. Guyot.

16.8   Cross Guyot Spur. Elevation here is 6,360 feet, the highest point on A.T. in eastern part of Great Smokies but 261 feet below summit of Mt. Guyot. From last gap, there has been net ascent of 290 feet.

17.4   Reach Guyot Spring.

17.9   Cross Pinnacle Lead, a spur off Tennessee side of Old Black. Pinnacle Lead forms boundary between Sevier and Cocke counties of Tennessee. From here to Davenport Gap, in the main, the Trail descends. Note pleasing view of English Mountain in Tennessee and of valley sections at foot of Great Smokies.

18.3   Enter Hell Ridge, named partly because of the devastation resulting from forest fire on North Carolina side along four-mile section of ridge, following timbering operations.

18.5   Follow state line through Deer Creek Gap (6,020 feet), with good views, particularly of Mt. Guyot, Luftee Knob, Balsam Corner, and Mt. Sterling, with their sharply de-fined ridges reaching down to Big Creek.

19.1   Reach Yellow Creek Gap. Swing around slope of Inadu Knob (5,941 feet). "Inadu" means "snake" in Cherokee and refers to snake dens on the mountainside.

19.4   Keep straight ahead at junction with trail on Tennessee side. (Trail to left, Snake Den Ridge Trail, leads past Maddron Bald Trail and down Snake Den Mountain to **Cosby Campground.** A spring is about 0.8 mile down this trail; descent from A.T. to spring is gradual.) Swing to Tennessee side around wooded side of Camel Hump Knob (5,250 feet).

21.8   Reach Camel Gap (4,645 feet). Side trail on North Carolina side, Camel Gap Trail, leads down to Big Creek and Walnut Bottom. Pass around forested side of Ross Knob (5,025 feet) on Tennessee side.

22.5   Forest growth on Tennessee side changes from coniferous to deciduous, largely oaks, beeches, maples, and a few chestnuts that survived the blight.

22.8   Pass around North Carolina side of Cosby Knob (5,145 feet). Trail passes out of fire-denuded Hell Ridge and through virgin forests on both sides.

23.3 **Cosby Knob Shelter** is 150 feet to right; accommodates 12; spring nearby.

23.4 Water crosses Trail.

24.0 Reach Low Gap (4,242 feet), having descended 758 feet from Cosby Knob. From Low Gap, side trails lead down into both states: On North Carolina side, Walnut Bottom Trail follows Low Gap Branch and then swings west near Walnut Bottom; on Tennessee side, Cosby Trail follows Cosby Creek 2.5 miles to **Cosby Campground.**

24.6 Cross crest of Rocky Face Mountain, spur on Tennessee side. In 0.5 mile, cross spur of Tennessee side of Sunup Knob (5,050 feet). Beyond are fine views in all directions.

25.9 After regaining 758 feet in ascent from Low Gap, cross high point (about 5,000 feet), and begin long descent toward Davenport Gap.

26.1 Where A.T. bears right, side trail continues ahead 0.6 mile along state line to tower on Mt. Cammerer, formerly White Rock, at eastern end of Great Smokies.

26.6 Pass spring. Just beyond, uphill, is small site used as a camp by the CCC during the construction of Mt. Cammerer tower.

28.1 Pass through gap in spur off North Carolina side of Mt. Cammerer. Descending along side of high rock cliff is spectacular Trail construction.

28.2 Side trail leads right 50 yards to spring.

28.5 Lower Mt. Cammerer Trail from **Cosby Campground,** 7.8 miles away, comes in on Tennessee side.

29.4 Chestnut Branch Trail leads 2.0 miles to Big Creek Ranger Station and **campground.**

30.4 Pass trail leading 100 yards left to **Davenport Gap Shelter;** accommodates 12; spring nearby.

31.1 Water is located to right and below Trail.

31.3 Reach Davenport Gap (1,975 feet) at northeastern end of Great Smoky Mountains National Park and end of section. To continue on A.T., follow N.C. 284 (Tenn. 32) 20 yards to right, cross highway, and take Trail up ramp. (See *Appalachian Trail Guide to Tennessee-North Carolina.*)

Newfound Gap (U.S. 441) to
Little Tennessee River (Fontana Dam)
Section Two
39.7 miles

Brief Description of Section

This section of the Trail, from the northern end at Newfound Gap to Clingmans Dome (7.9 miles), was constructed by the CCC in 1939-40. This portion of the Trail generally follows the state line on the crest of the ridges and lies on the northern side of the highway that was constructed from Newfound Gap to the Forney Ridge parking area on the southern slope of Clingmans Dome. The highway is rarely visible from the Trail. This link replaces an earlier route that had become unsatisfactory after the road's construction.

From Clingmans Dome, the Trail follows the main crest of the Smokies to Silers Bald. West of Silers Bald, the Trail passes through several open gaps and bald knobs, the most prominent of which is Thunderhead. It was cleared as a fire trail by the NPS in 1931. Use of the Trail, even over the balds, has worn a footway that indicates the route. In addition, the route is marked with white-paint blazes.

Since the route generally follows the state line as far as Doe Knob, the slopes are designated as North Carolina and Tennessee.

The Trail leaves the crest of the Great Smokies 32.2 miles from Newfound Gap and turns south along a spur ridge, crossing Shuckstack to reach the Little Tennessee River at Fontana Dam.

Points of Interest

This section traverses the western half of the Great Smoky Mountains National Park and contains some of the finest peaks of the Great Smokies, the balds. Particularly impressive are Thunderhead and Spence Field. Views from the tower on Clingmans Dome, the highest peak in the Great Smokies (6,643 feet), from the balds, and from the firetower on Shuckstack are outstanding. Clingmans Dome is also the highest point on the entire A.T.

Beyond Clingmans Dome, in marked contrast to the coniferous forests of the eastern Great Smokies, the Trail passes through typical southern Appalachian hardwood forests. Some of the Trail is along a grass-grown ridge dotted with mature timber, affording delightful travel.

Situated in the center of a bowl of high surrounding mountains, Shuckstack has one of the most extraordinary outlooks in the southern Appalachians. The crestline of the Great Smokies from Thunderhead to Clingmans Dome is prominent. Hangover, southwest of the Great Smokies, is particularly impressive. To the south are the extensive high mountains of the Nantahala National Forest. Below is Fontana Lake.

Road Approaches

The northern end of the section is at Newfound Gap on the Tennessee-North Carolina state line. U.S. 441 crosses the gap 55 miles south of Knoxville, Tennessee; 16 miles south of Gatlinburg, Tennessee; and 20 miles north of Cherokee, North Carolina. No scheduled bus service is available through Newfound Gap.

The southern end of the section is at Fontana Dam on the Little Tennessee River. Fontana Village Resort (P.O. Box 68, Fontana Dam, NC 28733) is about three miles from Fontana Dam, with stores, restaurants, post office, pool and fitness center, and excellent accommodations available, including a hostel. The village is 39 miles west of Bryson City, North Carolina, *via* U.S. 19 for 14 miles and N.C. 28 for 25 miles. Fontana Village may also be reached by taking U.S. 129 south from Knoxville, Tennessee, 37 miles to Deals Gap on the Tennessee-North Carolina state line and then N.C. 28 east for nine miles. No bus service is available to Fontana Village.

Maps

Refer to Trails Illustrated's Great Smoky Mountains National Park Map with this guidebook for route navigation. For additional area detail, refer to USGS Clingmans Dome, North Carolina-Tennessee; Silers Bald, North Carolina-Tennessee; Thunderhead, North Carolina-Tennessee; Cades Cove, North Carolina-Tennessee; and Fontana Dam, North Carolina, quadrangles.

Shelters, Campsites, and Water

This section has eight shelters and 14 water sources. *Reservations are required at all shelters*. During drought, some springs in this section may be dry. The shelters are:

Miles from Newfound Gap	Shelter
4.5	Mt. Collins (0.5 mile on side trail)
10.8	Double Spring Gap
12.5	Silers Bald
18.0	Derrick Knob
24.3	Spence Field (250 yards on side trail)
26.8	Russell Field
29.4	Mollies Ridge
34.5	Birch Spring (100 yards on side trail)

On the TVA Fontana Dam reservation, just south of the dam in the next Trail section (0.7 mile), is the Fontana Dam Shelter, which accommodates 20 and has a picnic area. At the visitors center on top of the dam are showers, meals, and laundry facilities.

Public Accommodations and Supplies

Only restrooms are available at Newfound Gap. From the parking area at the crest of Newfound Gap, it is 16 miles to Gatlinburg, Tennessee, which has a full range of motels, restaurants, and sources of supplies. The park headquarters is located two miles west of Gatlinburg.

Fontana Village Resort (Fontana Dam, NC 28733) is three miles from the southern end of this section, with stores, restaurants, laundry services, post office, hostel, and accommodations.

History

At Indian Gap, trail-like remnants of an old road built by Colonel William Thomas during the Civil War with Indian labor cross the Trail and the state line. This is the original transmountain road. It was built for obtaining saltpeter from Alum Cave Bluff, in an unsuccessful attempt to supply Confederate armies then under siege in eastern Virginia.

The correct location of Mt. Collins was once a subject of some controversy. An early USGS map had placed Mt. Collins east of Indian Gap (presently Mt. Kephart). Considering the peak between Indian Gap and Clingmans Dome as nameless, Asheville citizens sponsored a movement to name it Mt. Kephart in honor of Horace Kephart, noted authority on the southern Appalachians. An Arnold Guyot manuscript and map disclosed that this peak had been originally named Mt. Collins, and this name was restored. At the suggestion of the Tennessee Nomenclature Committee, the U.S. Geographic Board applied the name Kephart to the prominent peak three miles east of Newfound Gap.

Meigs Post was once about 0.2 mile west of the summit of Mt. Collins. This was the starting point of Return J. Meigs' survey in 1802, the exact location of which, whether at this point or at Miry Ridge, was an issue in litigation involving the ownership of extensive timber lands.

Clingmans Dome was formerly known as Smoky Dome. It was renamed for Thomas Lanier Clingman, U.S. senator, mining prospector, and Civil War general who explored those mountains during the 1850s and extolled their virtues.

The Bote Mountain Trail is the old Anderson Road. The road derives its name from the founder and former president of Maryville College, who promoted the construction of this road from Tuckaleechee Cove up Bote Mountain to the state line. The word "bote" designates the ridge that the majority of the Cherokee Indian labor force building the road voted the route should follow. Having no "v" sound in their language, they indicated their choice by saying "bote."

Precautions

This section is 39.7 miles long, but, because of its many ascents and descents, allow at least three days for its traverse. The route is easier to hike north to south because of the large difference in elevation between the two ends of the section.

Across the balds, the route is unmistakable in clear weather, but, when it is cloudy, foggy, or dark, it is necessary to watch paint blazes.

Trail Description, North to South

Miles	Data

0.0   From junction of Newfound Gap Road (U.S. 441) and the Trail from Davenport Gap, cross parking area to its western end, and descend through opening in guard wall at northwest side of parking area. Follow graded trail, paralleling Clingmans Dome Road, which extends 7.6 miles to Forney Ridge parking area on southern slope of Clingmans Dome. Highway is to the left. Pass rock retaining wall on left.

0.5   Continue straight ahead, where abandoned Thomas Ridge Trail leads left through tunnel under road. Ascend along Tennessee slope through beech-and-spruce forest.

0.9   At ridgetop, old trail (former A.T.) comes in on left. Beyond, ascend slope of Mt. Mingus with view of Mt. LeConte through balsam trees to right.

1.2   Reach ridgecrest of Mt. Mingus; follow crest, and bear left. (Obscure trail to right leads to summit of Mt. Mingus, 5,802 feet.) From crest, descend North Carolina slope through balsam, with glimpse of road 100 feet to left.

1.6   Turn sharply left, after bearing right across state line.

1.7   Reach Indian Gap, and cross grassy open slope on Tennessee side. Enter woods on western slope, and ascend Tennessee side, following graded trail. (Road from Newfound Gap to parking area on slope of Clingmans Dome is on crest to left; fine view of North Carolina side. Old road crosses Trail here. On Tennessee side, old road is known as Road Prong Trail. It is 3.3 miles on Road Prong to Newfound Gap Road at Chimneys parking area.)

1.8   Turn sharply left onto state-line ridge.

1.9   Keep right; left is old trail along crest.

2.2   Reach Little Indian Gap. Follow state-line ridge for next 1.9 miles.

4.1   Reach junction with a connector leading left 35 yards to Clingmans Dome Road and Fork Ridge Trail.

4.5   Reach junction of Sugarland Mountain Trail. Trail to right leads down 0.5 mile to **Mt. Collins Shelter**; accommodates 12; compost privy; spring nearby.

5.0   Reach summit of Mt. Collins (6,188 feet). Descend gradually and then steeply from Mt. Collins.

5.6   Reach Collins Gap (5,886 feet). Trail on Tennessee slope skirts road, which is on state line.

6.7   Reach summit of Mt. Love (6,446 feet), then descend into gap (6,366 feet) at eastern base of Clingmans Dome. Beyond, ascend steeply to summit.

7.9   Reach Clingmans Dome (6,643 feet), highest point on A.T. Rare mountain cranberry is abundant here. (Side trail to left leads 50 yards to observation tower, providing a splendid view above red-spruce and scattered fir trees. From tower, paved path leads downhill 0.5 mile to Forney Ridge parking area at end of road, 7.6 miles from Newfound Gap.) Continue ahead, then descend slightly along narrow ridgecrest to gap at northern base of Mt. Buckley, with fine view over East, or Main, Prong of Little River on Tennessee side. Mt. LeConte is most prominent peak visible here.

8.3   Reach wide trail on left. This is Clingmans Dome Bypass Trail, leading 1.0 mile to Forney Ridge Trail, where it is 1.5 miles to Andrews Bald and 11.5 miles to Fontana Lake; also leads to Forney Ridge parking area. Andrews Bald is one of two balds in the park maintained to remain grassy, open areas.

8.4   Ascend to summit of Mt. Buckley (6,582 feet). Descend steeply for 0.2 mile, then follow along ridge at head of Steel Trap Creek on North Carolina side (burned over in 1925).

8.8   Follow narrow ridgecrest.

10.2   On Tennessee side, pass junction of Goshen Prong Trail (leads to Goshen Prong of Little River and 10 miles to Elkmont campground and visitors center). Descend slightly.

10.8   Reach Double Spring Gap (5,507 feet) and **Double Spring Gap Shelter**; accommodates 12; privy. Gap is named for two unreliable springs, one on each slope; the better one is 15 yards from crest on North Carolina slope, while the other is 35 yards on Tennessee side. From gap, ascend through beech woods toward open knob east of Silers Bald. Beyond, vegetation changes: Spruce and fir growth becomes less dense and is succeeded by hardwoods, mainly beech.

11.3 Cross Jenkins Knob. Ahead is magnificent view of Silers Bald with Welch Ridge and High Rocks to left, Miry Ridge to right, and Thunderhead in background. Beyond this knob, few conifers are seen along Trail. Follow narrow, semiopen crest, crossing "The Narrows," where Trail takes a devious course along ridgecrest, dropping a short distance down on Tennessee side to avoid ledges. Ascend through dense beech growth.

12.1 Take less-worn right fork uphill along backbone of ridge. (Left is graded Welch Ridge Trail, which leads 7.5 miles to High Rocks and 16 miles to Fontana Lake at Hazel Creek. Exercise care here.) Ascend on switchbacks through dense woods.

12.3 Reach open crest of Silers Bald (5,607 feet) and panoramic view. Silers Bald is named for Siler family, who pastured cattle on it in summer, driving them up Welch Ridge. From crest, bear slightly left along open slope, and then bear right, descending along path through narrow, open field.

12.5 At edge of woods, trail to right leads 100 yards to spring. Just beyond this trail, pass **Silers Bald Shelter** on right; accommodates 12. Beyond shelter, follow ridgecrest through beech woods.

15.2 Descend steeply to Buckeye Gap (4,817 feet). Faint trails on both sides; water is 200 yards down North Carolina slope.

15.4 Reach graded Miry Ridge Trail on right, which leads 8.2 miles to public road at Elkmont, former summer resort. Stay on left fork.

16.0 Cross Cold Spring Knob (5,240 feet).

17.5 Skirt North Carolina slope of Mt. Davis, formerly known as Greenbrier Knob. Descend.

17.8 Reach Sams Gap (4,840 feet). Graded Greenbrier Ridge Trail comes in on right, leading *via* Middle Prong Trail 8.3 miles to public road above Tremont Ranger Station. A

	good spring is 100 yards down and to left on Greenbrier Ridge Trail.
17.9	Cross spur of knob, and enter open field at far corner of Tennessee side.
18.0	Pass **Derrick Knob Shelter** on right; accommodates 12; spring nearby. Shelter is located where herder's cabin once stood. Water is 50 yards to right on Tennessee slope. Cross overgrown field.
18.1	Enter woods at far corner of field. From Derrick Knob Shelter to Thunderhead, Trail is more strenuous.
18.3	Cross Chestnut Bald.
19.1	Reach Sugar Tree Gap (4,435 feet). Note sugar maples.
19.9	Enter Starkey Gap (4,500 feet); now wooded, it was grassy.
20.7	Bear left along North Carolina slope of wooded Brier Knob (5,215 feet), and descend.
20.8	Pass ledge with view into North Carolina; go into semiopen sag. Descend steeply along worn trail, skirting Tennessee slope of knob.
21.5	Enter Mineral Gap (5,030 feet).
22.2	Enter Beechnut Gap. Water is located 75 yards down Tennessee slope.
22.5	Ascend through laurel and rhododendron toward eastern summit of Thunderhead. Reach summit of Thunderhead (5,527 feet). (Triangulation marker is here.) Shortly after, come onto open ridge, and descend gradually with woods on left. Follow open ridgecrest. Trail leads for some two miles along open, grass-grown crest, interspersed with wooded sections. Route on worn path is unmistakable in clear weather, but it is necessary to watch paint blazes on rocks when vision is restricted by fog or darkness. Views from Thunderhead are outstanding.
23.1	Cross Rockytop (5,441 feet), which has views of Fontana Lake. Descend between jutting boulders, and bear right. Reach peak, and turn right down slope. Watch carefully for this turn, particularly in foggy or rainy weather.
23.9	In grassy sag, Jenkins Ridge Trail leads left 6.0 miles to the Lakeshore Trail at Pickens Gap. Follow right fork from intersection.
24.3	Pass Bote Mountain Trail on right, which is an excellent connection between Cades Cove and the A.T. Spring is 0.2

mile below A.T., beside Bote Mountain Trail. From junction with Bote Mountain Trail, bear left, and ascend field with splendid views. Spence Field is often considered the western end of Thunderhead. Almost immediately, pass Eagle Creek Trail, which leads left eight miles to Fontana Lake. **Spence Field Shelter** is 250 yards down this trail on Spence Cabin Branch of Gunna Creek, tributary of Eagle Creek; accommodates 12; spring nearby. Enter woods, and follow wide trail through sparse timber toward Little Bald. Travelling can be very rewarding in this section.

25.4   Reach Little Bald. Turn left through meadow (splendid southern views), and, after 70 yards, turn right. Continue across meadow, and enter woods.

26.5   Enter open McCampbell Gap (4,328 feet), and, at edge of woods at far end of clearing, skirt North Carolina side of wooded McCampbell Knob.

26.8   Reach eastern end of Russell Field. (Graded Russell Field Trail to right leads 4.8 miles to Cades Cove Picnic Area *via* Anthony Creek Trail.) **Russell Field Shelter** is located at trail intersection; accommodates 14; spring is 150 yards down trail toward Cades Cove. Skirt North Carolina side of Russell Field in woods.

27.3   Enter Big Abrams Gap (4,080 feet).

27.5   Reach top of knob, then descend steeply.

27.7   Enter Little Abrams Gap (4,120 feet). Ascend, switching back to grass-grown trail toward summit of Locust Knob.

29.1   Cross Devils Tater Patch (4,775 feet).

29.4   Reach **Mollies Ridge Shelter**; accommodates 12; spring nearby. Trail descends gradually then turns left onto a 1997 relocation skirting the western slope of Short Ridge.

30.8   Reach Ekaneetlee Gap (3,842 feet), through which passed an early Cherokee route from valley towns to overhill towns. Abandoned trail to right, Ekaneetlee Branch Trail, leads to Cades Cove in 5.8 miles. Water is found 100 yards down Tennessee slope. From gap, ascend toward Powell Knob on worn trail, bearing right.

31.6   Begin to skirt North Carolina side of Powell Knob (4,439 feet).

31.8   Reach Mud Gap (4,260 feet). Within 50 yards, leave gap, and ascend Doe Knob.

32.2   Reach summit of Doe Knob (4,520 feet). (Reach intersection with Gregory Bald Trail, which leads 3.1 miles to Gregory Bald, passing Rich Gap and intersection with Gregory Ridge Trail at 2.0 miles.) Major change in route begins. Trail leaves crest of Great Smokies and turns south along spur ridge, crossing Shuckstack Mountain to reach Little Tennessee River at Fontana Dam. Original A.T. route continued west over Gregory and Parson balds to Deals Gap.

32.3   Begin descent along spur ridge, with deep ravine on left. Beyond are outstanding views of crestline of Smokies from Thunderhead to Clingmans Dome. Ahead, Greer Knob is prominent.

32.9   Begin skirting right (western) slope of Greer Knob.

33.6   Return to ridgecrest on southern slope of Greer Knob, and descend for 250 feet.

33.7   Reach gap; water is located 100 yards down slope on right. From gap, follow narrow ridgecrest.

34.5   Reach Birch Spring Gap (3,834 feet). **Birch Spring Shelter** is 100 yards to right down slope; accommodates 12; spring nearby. Ahead is view of Shuckstack Mountain firetower. From gap, ascend steeply for 400 feet, then follow ridgecrest, and descend.

34.8   Reach Red Ridge Gap.

35.4   Reach Sassafras Gap (3,653 feet). To left, Lost Cove Trail leads 3.5 miles to Eagle Creek and the Lakeshore Trail. To right, gravel road leads to Twentymile Creek and to N.C. 28 at point 3.7 miles from Deals Gap on U.S. 129. From Sassafras Gap, follow south toward prominent firetower on Shuckstack Mountain (4,020 feet).

35.7   Reach ridgecrest. To left, old road leads 0.1 mile to fire warden's cabin and firetower on crest of Shuckstack. Firetower, by virtue of location on high side spur, allows one of the most extraordinary panoramic views of southern Appalachians. Crestline of Great Smokies from Thunderhead to Clingmans Dome is prominent. Hangover to southeast and mountains to south in Nantahala National Forest are particularly impressive. Tower overlooks Fontana Lake. Continue straight ahead, descending, on trail constructed by NPS in 1963.

35.9	Turn sharply left. Fantastic views ahead to south.
36.5	Reach gap between Shuckstack and Little Shuckstack. Skirt around western side of Little Shuckstack.
36.8	At bend in Trail, unreliable water source is a few yards to left.
36.9	Reach ridgecrest, and turn right, descending gradually.
38.8	Unreliable spring is 10 yards to right.
39.1	Reach hard-surfaced road. Turn right along road, and almost immediately reach intersection with dirt road (abandoned N.C. 288). Continue through intersection, and follow hard-surfaced road along lakeshore for 0.6 mile to northern end of Fontana Dam.
39.7	At northern end of dam, hard-surfaced road leads downstream 0.2 mile to parking overlook, which has spectacular view of dam and powerhouse from above. To continue on A.T., turn left onto roadway across dam, past visitors center (showers and toilets) in 0.4 mile. **Fontana Dam Shelter** is in woods on left, 0.3 mile south of visitors center (see Section Three, page 76).

Trail Description, South to North

Miles	Data
0.0	From end of Fontana Dam on northern bank of Little Tennessee River, follow hard-surfaced road to right along lakeshore for 0.6 mile. (To left, road leads downstream 0.2 mile to parking overlook, which has spectacular view of dam and powerhouse.)
0.6	Reach intersection with dirt, abandoned N.C. 288. On far side of intersection, turn left off hard-surfaced road, and enter woods. Graded trail, constructed by NPS in 1963, ascends Shuckstack Ridge gradually.
0.9	Unreliable spring is 10 yards to left. Ascend.
2.7	Shuckstack firetower is visible ahead.
2.8	Begin skirting western side of Little Shuckstack.
2.9	At bend of Trail, unreliable water is few yards to right.
3.2	Reach gap between Little Shuckstack and Shuckstack.
3.6	Excellent southern view.
3.8	Turn sharply right, ascending.

4.0   Reach ridgecrest. To right, road leads 0.1 mile to NPS cabin and firetower on Shuckstack, 4,020 feet. A.T. continues straight ahead. Firetower, by virtue of location on high side spur, allows one of the most extraordinary panoramic views of southern Appalachians. Crestline of Great Smokies from Thunderhead to Clingmans Dome is prominent. Hangover to southeast and mountains to south in Nantahala National Forest are particularly impressive. Tower overlooks Fontana Lake.

4.3   Reach Sassafras Gap (3,653 feet). To right, Lost Cove Trail leads 3.5 miles to Eagle Creek and the Lakeshore Trail. To left, gravel road leads to N.C. 28 at a point 3.7 miles from Deals Gap on U.S. 129.

4.6   Reach ridgecrest, and ascend, then descend for 0.2 mile.

4.9   Reach Red Ridge Gap, ascend, and follow ridgecrest.

5.2   Reach Birch Spring Gap (3,834 feet). To left, 100 yards down slope on worn trail, is **Birch Spring Shelter**; accommodates 12; spring nearby.

6.1   Reach gap at southern base of Greer Knob. Spring is 100 yards to left down slope. From gap, ascend for 250 feet along crest.

6.2   Skirt western slope of Greer Knob for next 0.6 mile.

7.2   Reach sag at base of main crest of Great Smokies, and ascend steeply.

7.5   Reach ridgecrest. Turn sharply right, and reach Doe Knob in 400 feet. Doe Knob (4,520 feet) is on crest of Great Smokies. Route turns right, east, and follows ridgecrest for 32.2 miles to Newfound Gap. (On left, Gregory Bald Trail, part of the original A.T., comes in, 3.1 miles from Gregory Bald.) From Doe Knob, follow along level crest for 0.1 mile, then descend.

7.9   Reach Mud Gap (4,260 feet), then skirt North Carolina side of Powell Knob (4,439 feet).

8.1   Descend gradually for 0.7 mile.

8.9   Reach Ekaneetlee Gap (3,842 feet), through which passed an early Cherokee route from valley towns to overhill towns. Abandoned trail to left leads 5.8 miles to Cades Cove. Water is 100 yards down Tennessee slope. Ascend gradually from Ekaneetlee Gap on a 1997 trail relocation for 0.8 mile skirting the ridge (eastern) slope of Short

Ridge. Beyond, continue to ascend gradually along open ridge through sparse timber on wide trail.

10.3   Reach **Mollies Ridge Shelter;** accommodates 12; spring nearby.

10.6   Cross Devils Tater Patch (4,775 feet), and follow open, grassy ridgecrest.

10.8   Cross Locust Knob.

12.0   Reach Little Abrams Gap (4,120 feet), and ascend steeply.

12.4   Reach Big Abrams Gap (4,080 feet), and ascend steadily.

12.5   Skirt North Carolina side of Russell Field in woods below edge of field.

12.9   At far end of Russell Field, bear right. Graded Russell Field Trail to left leads 4.8 miles to Cades Cove picnic area *via* Anthony Creek Trail. **Russell Field Shelter** is at trail intersection; accommodates 14; spring 150 yards down trail to Cades Cove.

13.2   Reach grassy McCampbell Gap (4,328 feet).

14.3   Reach edge of meadow (Little Bald) with excellent southern views. Turn left for 70 yards, and leave meadow. Turn right, and enter woods. Follow along flat crest through open woods, descending slightly, and enter grassy Spence Field, often considered the western end of Thunderhead. Splendid views. From Spence Field, Trail passes for two miles along Thunderhead. Route on worn path is unmistakable in clear weather, but watch paint blazes on rocks when vision is restricted by fog or darkness.

15.4   Keep left. Eagle Creek Trail on right leads eight miles to Fontana Lake. **Spence Field Shelter** is 250 yards down this trail on Spence Cabin Branch of Gunna Creek, tributary of Eagle Creek; accommodates 12; privy; spring nearby. Almost immediately on left, pass graded Bote Mountain Trail, which connects to Cades Cove in 4.9 miles and Laurel Creek Road in 7.2 miles. A spring is 0.2 mile below A.T., beside Bote Mountain Trail. Keep slightly to right in open Spence Field; splendid views. Descend steeply.

15.8   Enter grassy sag. Jenkins Ridge Trail to right leads 6.0 miles to Lakeshore Trail at Pickens Gap. From sag, ascend grassy, overgrown slope.

16.6   Reach summit of Rockytop (5,441 feet), and ascend between jutting boulders. View of Fontana Lake.

17.2   Reach rhododendron-clad summit of Thunderhead (5,527 feet). Triangulation marker is here.

17.5   Reach Beechnut Gap. Water is 75 yards down Tennessee slope.

18.2   Reach Mineral Gap (5,030 feet).

18.9   Pass through semiopen sag, and then pass ledge with fine views of North Carolina side.

19.0   Swing around North Carolina slope of wooded Brier Knob (5,215 feet). No trail to summit. Return to crest, and descend very steeply.

19.8   Reach Starkey Gap (4,500 feet), formerly grassy, now wooded. Climb gradually along North Carolina slope.

20.6   Enter Sugar Tree Gap (4,435 feet). Note sugar maples here. Ascend along crest.

21.2   Pass through slight gap with good views of North Carolina.

21.4   Cross Chestnut Bald, with views on North Carolina slope.

21.6   Enter overgrown field.

21.7   Reach **Derrick Knob Shelter**; accommodates 12; spring nearby. Shelter is located where herder's cabin used to stand. Keep left. Beyond shelter, enter woods.

21.9   Enter Sams Gap (4,840 feet). Take right fork. Left is graded Greenbrier Ridge Trail, which leads 8.3 miles down to public road *via* Middle Prong Trail above Tremont Ranger Station. A good spring is 100 yards down and to left of Greenbrier Ridge Trail. Continue along crest.

22.2   Swing around North Carolina side of Mt. Davis, formerly Greenbrier Knob.

23.7   Reach Cold Spring Knob (5,240 feet).

24.3   Pass Miry Ridge Trail on left, which leads 9.2 miles to Elkmont, former summer resort.

24.5   Reach Buckeye Gap (4,817 feet). Faint trails here on both sides; water may be found about 200 yards down North Carolina slope. Follow crest, alternately climbing and descending gradually through beech woods.

27.0   Reach **Silers Bald Shelter**; accommodates 12. Just beyond shelter, trail to left leads 100 yards to spring. Beyond side trail to spring, bear left.

27.2 Cross crest of Silers Bald (5,607 feet). Silers Bald is named for family who pastured cattle on it in summer, driving them up Welch Ridge. Good view of Mt. LeConte on Tennessee side. To south is Welch Ridge; to east is good view of Clingmans Dome; high mountains are visible in all directions. Descend on switchbacks to east.

27.5 Enter beech woods.

27.6 Pass Welch Ridge Trail on North Carolina side (leads about 7.5 miles to High Rocks and 16 miles to Fontana Lake). Continue on well-worn trail, passing through two small, grassy meadows with good views of Silers Bald and other mountains.

28.4 Reach Jenkins Knob. Use care here. Keep well to left, entering woods about 100 feet before reaching summit of Jenkins Knob. Descend gradually.

28.9 Reach Double Spring Gap (5,507 feet) and **Double Spring Gap Shelter**; accommodates 12. Name of gap refers to two unreliable springs, one on each side of state line. Better spring is on North Carolina side, 15 yards from actual crest; on Tennessee side, the other is 35 yards from crest. Both springs flow into Tennessee River. From Double Spring Gap, ascend slightly.

29.5 Pass on left (Tennessee) side junction of Goshen Prong Trail, which leads to Goshen Prong of Little River and, in 10 miles, to Elkmont.

31.1 Climb through clearing in old fire scar on North Carolina side of slope at head of Steel Trap Creek, reentering virgin forest.

31.3 Cross summit of Mt. Buckley (6,582 feet). Reach gap at northern base of Mt. Buckley, with fine view of East, or Main, Prong of Little River on Tennessee side. Mt. LeConte is very prominent.

31.4 Pass wide trail on right. This is Clingmans Dome Bypass Trail, leading 1.0 mile to Forney Ridge Trail, from which it is 1.5 miles to Andrews Bald and 11.5 miles to Fontana Lake; also leads to Forney Ridge parking area. Andrews Bald is one of two balds in the park being preserved as open grassy meadows. Continue along crest.

31.8 Reach Clingmans Dome (6,643 feet), highest point on A.T. Rare mountain cranberry is abundant here. Side trail to right leads 50 yards to observation tower, which provides splendid view above red spruce and scattered firs. From tower, hard-surfaced path leads downhill 0.5 mile to Forney Ridge parking area at end of Clingmans Dome Road, 7.6 miles from Newfound Gap. From Clingmans Dome on Trail, descend steeply into a gap. Beyond, ascend.

33.0   Reach summit of Mt. Love (6,446 feet), then descend gradually.

34.1   Reach Collins Gap (5,886 feet). Beyond, ascend steeply; fine views.

34.7   Reach summit of Mt. Collins (6,188 feet). Summit overgrown; 100 feet before reaching summit is partial view over North Carolina side. From summit, descend.

35.2   Sugarland Mountain Trail comes in on left. **Mt. Collins Shelter** is 0.5 mile down this trail. Built-in bunks accommodate 12; spring nearby.

35.6   Trail to right leads 35 yards to Dome Road and Fork Ridge Trails.

37.5   Reach Little Indian Gap, and then ascend.

38.0   Reach Indian Gap. Old road crosses state line here. On Tennessee side, old road is known as Road Prong Trail; it leads 3.3 miles to Chimneys parking area on Newfound Gap Road (U.S. 441).

38.5   Bear right. Old, obscure trail leading to summit of Mt. Mingus (5,802 feet) leads to left.

38.8   Reach crest of Mt. Mingus Ridge. Beyond, descend slope, with views of Mt. LeConte through balsam trees to left. Descend along Tennessee slope through beech and spruce forest.

39.2   Continue ahead where abandoned Thomas Ridge Trail to right leads through tunnel under road. Continue on Trail, paralleling road and rock retaining wall on right.

39.7   Reach parking area on U.S. 441 at crest of ridge in Newfound Gap. Cross parking area to Trail on opposite (eastern) side, which has magnificent panoramic view. Particularly noteworthy is the Balsam Range, "master" crosschain of Great Smokies.

Side Trails in Great Smoky Mountains National Park

Side trails in this chapter include all the trails that branch directly from the A.T. and most of those that diverge from them as well. The listing begins at the northeastern end of the park at Davenport Gap and proceeds southwest to Fontana Dam. This covers a large part, but not all, of the 900-mile network of trails in the Great Smoky Mountains National Park. Detailed descriptions of more than 500 trails in the park are given in the *Hiker's Guide to the Smokies* by Dick Murlless and Constance Stallings (Sierra Club, 1973). While this particular book is out of print, it can still be found in libraries.

Most of the side trails are standard four-foot graded paths; a few are narrower, graded foot trails; others substandard. They may be good or quite rough in places and might be overgrown in the summer. With the discontinuance of the CCC decades ago, inadequate appropriations and consequent lack of personnel have meant curtailing much of the Trail maintenance in the Smokies. Even some of the less-used "grade A" trails may be overgrown in summer or still affected by cumulative storm damage.

Trails originating at the A.T. are numbered and referred to as leading north (into Tennessee) or south (into North Carolina), although they do not necessarily follow those compass directions. Where such trails do not originate at a point named in the guide, a distance is given from the nearest named point. The diverging trails are lettered as subdivisions of the side trails from which they branch; their beginnings are marked by distances from the A.T.

1. *Chestnut Branch Trail.* Leads south 2.0 miles to Big Creek Road near ranger station and primitive campground.

2. *Lower Mt. Cammerer Trail.* Leaves A.T. 2.8 miles west of Davenport Gap; leads north 7.4 miles to public road at Cosby Campground on easy grade, going around northern side of Mt. Cammerer through younger forest growth.

3. *Mt. Cammerer Trail.* Leaves A.T. 5.2 miles west of Davenport Gap; leads northeast 0.6 mile along crest to newly refurbished Mt.

Cammerer firetower. Passes through rhododendron, laurel, and azalea and over bare rock.

4. *Low Gap Trail.* Crosses A.T. at Low Gap; leads north 2.5 miles to public road at Cosby Campground. Passes through sourwood, hickory, oak, red maple, birch, and, toward lower end, some large virgin hemlock and tulip trees. Also leads south 2.5 miles along Low Gap Branch to Big Creek Trail, at Walnut Bottom; then down Big Creek Trail 5.1 miles to Big Creek Primitive Campground near Mountain Mama's. Section from Walnut Bottom to campground is on an old road.

5. *Camel Gap Trail.* Leaves A.T. at Camel Gap; leads 10.2 miles to Big Creek Primitive Campground near Mt. Sterling community and Mountain Mama's. There are good views of Big Creek watershed. The last 5.1 miles from Walnut Bottom is on Big Creek Trail.

6. *Snake Den Ridge Trail.* Leaves A.T. 2.3 miles west of Camel Gap on eastern slope of Inadu Knob; leads north 5.3 miles to Cosby Campground. First mile is through eastern-hemlock forest.

6-A. *Maddron Bald Trail.* Leaves No. 6 at 0.7 mile north of A.T.; crosses Maddron Bald and leads 7.2 miles to Laurel Springs Road to Hwy. 321.

7. *Balsam Mountain Trail.* Leaves A.T. at Tricorner Knob; leads south 10.1 miles to Pin Oak Gap, where it intersects Balsam Mountain Road. Open to one-way motor travel from Heintooga to Round Bottom, May through October. Left on this road, Balsam Mountain Campground is 8.5 miles; to right, public road at Round Bottom on Straight Fork is five miles. Laurel Gap Shelter is seven miles from A.T. *via* this trail; accommodates 14, spring nearby.

7-A. *Gunter Fork Trail.* Leaves No. 7 at 5.6 miles south of A.T.; leads left five miles to Walnut Bottom—difficult stream crossings during high stream flow.

7-B. *Mt. Sterling Ridge Trail.* Leaves No. 7 at 6.5 miles south of A.T.; leads left 7.2 miles to N.C. 284 at Mt. Sterling Gap.

7-C. *Beech Gap Trail.* Leaves No. 7 at 8.5 miles south of A.T.; leads right 2.5 miles to public road at Round Bottom on Straight Fork.

8. *Hughes Ridge Trail.* Leaves A.T. at Pecks Corner; passes Pecks Corner Shelter on left; leads south 12.6 miles to public road at Smokemont Campground; 1.5 miles of trail is owned by the Cherokees, not maintained by Park. Route mostly through northern hardwoods; exceptional views of the Bradley Fork virgin-hardwood forest. Five miles down the trail is a fine stand of flame azalea.

8-A. *Bradley Fork Trail.* Leaves No. 8 at 2.2 miles south of A.T.; leads right 7.5 miles *via* Taywa Creek and Bradley Fork to public road at Smokemont Campground.

8-B. *Enloe Creek Trail.* Leaves No. 8 at 4.7 miles south of A.T.; leads left 3.6 miles to Hyatt Ridge Trail.

8-C. *Chasteen Creek Trail.* Leaves No. 8 at 4.7 miles south of A.T.; leads right 5.3 miles *via* Chasteen Creek and Bradley Fork to a public road at Smokemont Campground.

9. *Dry Sluice Gap Trail (formerly Richland Mountain Trail).* Leaves A.T. at Dry Sluice Gap; leads south 3.8 miles to Cabin Flats Trail *via* Bradley Fork Trail to public road at Smokemont.

9-A. *Grassy Branch Trail.* Leaves No. 9 at 1.3 miles south of A.T.; leads right 4.5 miles to U.S. 441 *via* Grassy Branch and Kephart Prong. Kephart Shelter is 3.8 miles from A.T. *via* this trail; accommodates 14; creek water.

10. *Boulevard Trail.* Leaves A.T. at crest of A.T. on shoulder of Mt. Kephart; leads north 5.3 miles to Mt. LeConte. This is a ridgecrest trail through spruce and fir with exceptional views of Porters Creek watershed. From points near LeConte's High Top, trails lead to Myrtle Point and to Cliff Top, with spectacular views. Many of LeConte's ledges are covered with dwarf rhododendron and sand myrtle. A lodge on Mt. LeConte is open from late March to middle November; primitive accommodations are available. (Write Wilderness Lodging, Sevierville, TN 37862, for information.) A shelter is beside the Boulevard Trail near LeConte's High Top; accommodates 12. Spring is down Trillium Gap Trail below LeConte Lodge; see below.

10-A. *Jumpoff Trail.* Leaves No. 10 at 0.1 mile north of A.T.; leads right 0.8 mile to the Jumpoff, rock ledge offering spectacular view into valleys of Porters Creek watershed, almost 1,000 feet below. Route also crosses summit at Mt. Kephart (6,200 feet). To reach the Jumpoff, cross summit of Mt. Kephart, and follow worn footway.

10-B. *Trillium Gap Trail.* From Mt. LeConte, leads 6.5 miles to Roaring Fork Motor-Nature Trail, open to one-way motor traffic from Cherokee Orchard down Roaring Fork, May till December 1. At 3.6 miles (Trillium Gap), turns left.

10-C. *Rainbow Falls Trail.* Leaves Mt. LeConte; leads 6.5 miles to public road at Cherokee Orchard. First section is down Rocky Spur, with excellent views of valleys to the north. Passes Rainbow Falls.

10-D. *Alum Cave Bluff Trail*. From Mt. LeConte, leads 5.2 miles to parking lot on U.S. 441 from Gatlinburg. At three miles, trail passes under Alum Cave Bluff; at 4.2 miles, through Arch Rock. From just below bluff, "needle's eye" can be seen in ridge off to right.

11. *Sweat Heifer Creek Trail*. Leaves A.T. one mile west of crest on shoulder of Mt. Kephart; leads south 5.8 miles to U.S. 441 *via* Sweat Heifer Creek and Kephart Prong. Leads through an area where disastrous fire occurred in 1995; Norway spruce, eastern hemlock, Fraser magnolias, and mountain laurel now grow here. Good views of Oconaluftee Valley. Kephart Shelter is beside this trail 3.7 miles from A.T.; accommodates 14; creek water.

12. *Road Prong Trail*. Leaves A.T. at Indian Gap; leads north 3.3 miles to U.S. 441 at Chimneys parking area. A historic trail, it is the original transmountain road. Constructed by Colonel William Thomas with Cherokee Indians during Civil War, for general war purposes and to obtain saltpeter from Alum Cave Bluff in an unsuccessful attempt to supply Confederate armies then under siege in eastern Virginia. Abundance of rhododendron among virgin hemlock and hardwoods in this area. Crosses Road Prong several times without footbridges.

12-A. *Chimneys Tops Trail*. Leaves No. 12 at 2.4 miles north of Trail; leads left about 1.1 miles to top of Chimneys.

13. *Fork Ridge Trail*. Leaves A.T. 0.9 mile east of Mt. Collins; leads south 14.7 miles to public road at Deep Creek Campground *via* Fork Ridge and Deep Creek to Bryson Place, 8.6 miles from A.T. First mile is through many dead Fraser fir, which have been killed by the balsam woody adelgid; to Deep Creek Gap, through northern hardwoods; and to Bryson Place, through virgin hardwoods.

14. *Sugarland Mountain Trail*. Leaves A.T. 0.5 mile east of Mt. Collins; leads north 12.1 miles to Little River Road at Fighting Creek Gap. Excellent views of Mt. LeConte and Sugarland and Little River valleys.

14-A. *Rough Creek Trail*. Leaves No. 14 about 4.8 miles from A.T.; leads left 5.0 miles to public road one mile south of Elkmont. Lower three miles is on old road.

14-B. *Huskey Gap Trail*. Crosses No. 14 at about 9 miles from A.T.; leads left 2.1 miles to Little River Trail south of Elkmont. Leads right 2.0 miles to Newfound Gap Road.

15. *Clingmans Dome Trail.* Leads 50 yards to tower and then on a paved path 0.5 mile downhill to Forney Ridge parking area at the end of Clingmans Dome Road, 7.6 miles from Newfound Gap.

16. *Clingmans Dome Bypass Trail.* Leads 1.0 mile to Forney Ridge Trail, which begins at the end of Clingmans Dome Road (road closed in winter).

17. *Forney Ridge Trail.* Leaves Forney Ridge parking area and leads 11.5 miles to Fontana Lake. Marvelous views of Forney Creek and Noland Creek valleys. At 1.5 miles, crosses Andrews Bald, with large mountain meadow. At lower end of meadow, turn sharply right. Unreliable spring is located on the lower end (southwestern corner) of Andrews Bald.

17-A. *Forney Creek Trail.* Leaves No. 17 at 1.0 mile south of Forney Ridge parking area; leads right 10.8 miles *via* Forney Creek to Fontana Lake; passes Forney Creek cascades. Last 4.0 miles are on gravel road.

17-B. *Springhouse Branch Trail.* Crosses No. 17 6.6 miles south of A.T.; leads left 3.0 miles to gravel road on Noland Creek and right 4.0 miles *via* Bee Gum Branch to Forney Creek Trail.

18. *Goshen Prong Trail.* Leaves A.T. 0.6 mile east of Double Spring Gap; leads north 10 miles to public road one mile south of Elkmont. The first 0.2 mile is through spruce; 1.2 miles is through rhododendron and hemlock; balance is through hardwoods. The last 2.3 miles are on the Little River Trail.

19. *Welch Ridge Trail.* Leaves A.T. 0.2 mile east of Silers Bald; leads south 7.5 miles on crest of Welch Ridge to High Rocks. Traverses second-growth hardwoods and offers views of adjacent valleys. Ends at Cold Spring Gap Trail.

19-A. *Hazel Creek Trail.* Leaves No. 19 1.5 miles south of A.T. and leads 14.0 miles *via* Hazel Creek and Lakeshore trails to Fontana Lake.

19-B. *Jonas Creek Trail.* Leaves No. 19 2.0 miles south of A.T.; leads left 4.5 miles to Forney Creek Trail. Follows Yanu Ridge and Jonas Creek.

19-C. *Bear Creek Trail.* Leaves No. 19 at 6.4 miles south of A.T.; leads left 6.8 miles to Fontana Lake. Follows Jumpup Ridge and Bear and Forney creeks.

20. *Miry Ridge Trail.* Leaves A.T. 0.2 mile west of Buckeye Gap; leads north 8.2 miles to public road at Elkmont. Follows Miry Ridge

and Dripping Springs Mountain to Jakes Gap and then down Jakes Creek Trail.

20-A. *Lynn Camp Prong Trail.* Leaves No. 20 at 2.5 miles north of A.T.; leads left 2.4 miles to Middle Prong Trail above Tremont Ranger Station. Lower end is on gravel road. Large laurel are seen on this trail.

20-B. *Blanket Mountain Trail.* Leaves No. 20 at Jakes Gap, 4.9 miles north of A.T.; leads ahead 0.8 mile to Blanket Mountain.

20-C. *Panther Creek Trail.* Leaves No. 20 at Jakes Gap 4.9 miles north of A.T.; leads left 2.2 miles to Middle Prong Trail above Tremont Ranger Station.

21. *Greenbrier Ridge Trail.* Leaves A.T. 0.2 mile east of Derrick Knob Shelter; leads north 8.3 miles *via* Middle Prong Trail to public road above Tremont Ranger Station. Route is through beech woods for 0.2 mile and then in cut-over area.

22. *Jenkins Ridge Trail.* Leaves A.T. at eastern end of Spence Field; leads 6.0 miles to Pickens Gap on Lakeshore Trail.

23. *Bote Mountain Trail.* Leaves A.T. near center of Spence Field; leads north 7.2 miles to Laurel Creek Road. First 0.5 mile is rocky through yellow birch; next 0.5 mile, through rhododendron tunnel with trail down to bedrock; next mile, laurel slick; balance, on old road through pine and hardwoods.

23-A. *Anthony Creek Trail.* Leaves No. 23 at 1.7 miles north of A.T.; leads left through hardwood forest 3.5 miles to campground and picnic area and onto public road in eastern end of Cades Cove. Lower end is on old road.

23-B. *Lead Cove Trail.* Leaves No. 23 at 2.9 miles and leads 1.8 miles to Laurel Creek Road.

23-C. *Finley Cane Trail.* Leaves No. 23 at 5.4 miles and leads 2.8 miles to Laurel Creek Road.

23-D. *West Prong Trail.* Leaves No. 23 at 6.0 miles north of A.T.; leads right 2.7 miles to public road on Middle Prong Little River, above Tremont Ranger Station.

24. *Eagle Creek Trail.* Leaves A.T. near center of Spence Field; leads south 8.0 miles to Fontana Lake.

25. *Russell Field Trail.* Leaves A.T. at Russell Field; leads north 5.1 miles to picnic area in eastern end of Cades Cove. First 0.5 mile is across grassy bald; then 0.5 mile through virgin hardwood forest; next mile, on pine ridge (Leadbetter Ridge); then down Right Prong of Anthony Creek, through beautiful forest of hemlock and

rhododendron. Dense and moss-covered growth gives tropical effect. Lower 1.6 miles is on Anthony Creek Trail, No. 23-A.

26. *Gregory Bald Trail.* Leaves A.T. at Doe Knob; leads right 7.2 miles to Parson Branch Road (open to one-way traffic from Cades Cove to U.S. 129 May through December). Route from Doe Knob to Sheep Pen Gap is portion of former A.T. in western Great Smokies abandoned when A.T. was relocated to cross Little Tennessee River at Fontana Dam. Passes through Rich Gap at 2.0 miles from the A.T. At 3.1 miles from A.T., Gregory Bald (4,948 feet) has, in late June, an outstanding display of azalea. About 200 acres comprise the bald, which has a fine panoramic view. Cherokee Indians called this bald "Tsistuyi," the "rabbit place," where the chief of the rabbits ruled. When settlers first came, they grazed sheep here. Great Smoky Mountains National Park maintains this and Andrews Bald as open areas by cutting new growth.

26-A. *Long Hungry Ridge Trail.* Leaves No. 26 at Rich Gap (also known as "Gant Lot," the mountaineers' name for where cattle were corralled to be "hardened up" or "gaunted … ga'nted" before being driven from the mountains); leads south eight miles *via* Twentymile Trail to N.C. 28, 3.7 miles from Deals Gap on U.S. 129. Follows Long Hungry Ridge, Rye Patch Branch, and Twentymile Creek. Lower 3.3 miles is on gravel road.

26-B. *Gregory Ridge Trail.* Leaves No. 26 at Rich Gap; leads north 4.9 miles to Forge Creek Road in western end of Cades Cove. Follows Gregory Ridge for about 2.2 miles and then descends and follows Ekaneetlee Branch and Forge Creek. On ridge, it passes through hardwoods and pine and, upon reaching branch, through some of the largest poplars and hemlocks in park.

26-C. *Wolf Ridge Trail.* Leaves No. 26 at 3.1 miles from A.T.; leads left about 0.8 mile to Parson Bald, a peak similar to Gregory Bald but smaller. Leads south 6.5 miles to Twentymile Trail, about 0.5 mile from ranger station and N.C. 28.

27. *Twentymile Trail.* Leaves A.T. at Sassafras Gap, 0.3 mile north of Shuckstack firetower side trail; leads right 5.0 miles to N.C. 28, 3.7 miles from Deals Gap on U.S. 129. Follows Proctor Branch and Twentymile Creek. Lower 3.3 miles is on gravel road.

28. *Lost Cove Trail.* Leaves A.T. at Sassafras Gap and leads left 3.5 miles to Eagle Creek and the Lakeshore Trail.

The Appalachian Trail in the
Nantahala National Forest
87.9 Miles

In the Nantahala National Forest (NNF), most of the A.T. passes through mature hardwood forest. Rhododendron, mountain laurel, flame azalea, mountain ash, fern, galax, wildflowers, streams, springs, and the fall coloring all contribute to the A.T. in the South being so distinctive an experience.

The Reverend Doctor A. Rufus Morgan, who helped establish and maintain the A.T. in North Carolina, described the area most eloquently:

"A trip in October will give opportunity of seeing grouse, wild turkeys, squirrels, deer, and occasionally other wildlife. The coloring, also, makes a fall trip a beautiful experience. Early October will give an abundance of wildflowers, such as asters, phlox, self-heal, and closed gentian.

"A spring trip, perhaps in late April, will show the white-flowering trees, such as dogwood, bellwood, service, and black locust. Along with these, the red maples show a beautiful contrast. Then there are the flowers.... The bluets furnish quite a carpet. There are violets in abundance, as well as the trilliums and trout lilies. The many varieties of fern present an interesting study... From Deep Gap to the Georgia line the interrupted fern grows in great profusion...During June and July...a wealth of flame azalea and rhododendron, especially the purple rhododendron on Standing Indian Mountain."

Many recreational facilities and places of historical importance are near Fontana Dam, the northernmost part of the A.T. in the NNF. (Details in Section Three.)

A rewarding trip from Fontana is to the Joyce Kilmer Memorial Forest, a reservation of magnificent trees 21.7 miles from the intersection of U.S. 129 with N.C. 28. An easy trail of about 1.5 miles leads past the Kilmer Memorial through superlative forest growth. Overnight camping is not permitted, but the USFS Horse Cove Campground is adjacent.

Trails to three outstanding mountains begin in the Joyce Kilmer Memorial Forest: Hangover Mountain (5,160 feet), Haoe (5,249 feet), and Stratton Bald (5,341 feet). For trails to Hangover and Snowbird mountains, see TVA Tapoco and Santeetlah Creek quadrangle maps and USFS Nantahala National Forest map. Also of interest is the Snowbird Range to the south. (See Nantahala National Forest map.)

The first part of the southbound A.T. parallels the Little Tennessee River. It heads east from near the western end of the Great Smokies to the northern end of the Nantahala Range. Particularly impressive are the panoramic views of the Great Smokies on one side and the Nantahala, Cowee, and Snowbird mountains on the other. The view from Cheoah Bald is one of the outstanding views of the southern Appalachians.

At the Nantahala River, the A.T. climbs out of Nantahala Gorge and proceeds over a series of 5,000-foot summits (heath balds characteristic of the southern Appalachians) and 4,000-foot gaps. It flanks the headwaters of the Nantahala, Little Tennessee, and Tallulah rivers. At Ridgepole Mountain, the end of the Nantahala Range, it turns to the eastern arm of the Blue Ridge for the remainder of its journey to Georgia.

The Appalachian Trail goes through historic country in western North Carolina. Before white settlers arrived in the eighteenth century, the area was inhabited by the Cherokee Nation. Explorer Hernando de Soto traveled from Nikwasi (the present-day Franklin) across the Nantahalas to Murphy in 1539. He must have passed through one of the gaps along the route of the Appalachian Trail.

In 1775, the naturalist William Bartram traveled an Indian trail from Nikwasi to the Nantahala River, hoping to reach the overhill towns in east Tennessee. The following year, General Rutherford, on a search-and-destroy mission against the Cherokee Indians, led his troops through Wayah Gap, fighting a skirmish there.

In 1819, a line separating Cherokee and white settlements was drawn along the crest of the Nantahalas.

"Old 64" in Wallace Gap follows the route of an Indian trading path that developed into a colonial road.

Siler Bald in the Nantahalas was named for an early settler, William Siler, great-grandfather of the late Rev. Morgan. Albert Mountain was named for Dr. Morgan's grandfather, Albert Siler.

Standing Indian Campground, situated on the headwaters of the Nantahala River, was the site of a lumber camp in the late nineteenth and early twentieth centuries.

The John B. Byrne Observation Tower (memorial to a former supervisor of the Nantahala National Forest who first proposed the route of the Appalachian Trail in this area) is located on Wayah Bald.

Recent relocations of the A.T., logging operations in the national forest, and drought have affected the springs and mountain streams of the southern mountains. *Always carry an emergency supply of drinking water, and treat water found along the Trail or by the shelters before using it.*

Camping is permitted in most of the national forest (prohibited areas are clearly marked by USFS signs). It is unnecessary to register for the 13 shelters along the route.

The section of A.T. from the Little Tennessee River to the Nantahala River (Wesser) is maintained by members of the Smoky Mountains Hiking Club, P.O. Box 1454, Knoxville, TN 37938. The sections from the Nantahala River (Wesser) to Bly Gap (near the North Carolina-Georgia state line) are maintained by members of the Nantahala Hiking Club, 31 Carl Slagle Road, Franklin, NC 28734.

The section from the Little Tennessee River to Bly Gap is in the Nantahala National Forest. From the Little Tennessee to the Nantahala, the Trail is in the Cheoah Ranger District, with offices in Robbinsville, North Carolina. From the Nantahala River to Deep Gap, the Trail is in the Wayah Ranger District, with offices in Franklin. The Deep Gap–Bly Gap section is the Tusquittee District, with offices in Murphy. Trail maintenance is also provided by USFS personnel.

This part of the guide has been divided into eight Trail sections. Each section has introductory material that describes the terrain, approaches, side trails, water sources, campsites, *etc.* Each section has detailed Trail data, with north-south and south-north mileages listed separately. This part concludes with a special section on side trails in the Nantahalas.

The eight sections are:

Section Three: Little Tennessee River (Fontana Dam) to Yellow Creek Gap, 8.2 miles.
Section Four: Yellow Creek Gap to Stecoah Gap, 7.6 miles.
Section Five: Stecoah Gap to the Nantahala River (Wesser), 13.6 miles.
Section Six: Nantahala River (Wesser) to Tellico Gap, 7.9 miles.
Section Seven: Tellico Gap to Wayah Gap, 13.5 miles.
Section Eight: Wayah Gap to Wallace Gap, 9.0 miles.
Section Nine: Wallace Gap to Deep Gap, 21.3 miles.
Section Ten: Deep Gap to Bly Gap, 6.8 miles.

Little Tennessee River (Fontana Dam) to Yellow Creek Gap
Section Three
8.2 miles

Brief Description of Section

The A.T. originally extended the length of the Great Smokies and used the only available crossing of the Little Tennessee River, at Tapoco, North Carolina. From that point, the Yellow Creek Mountains were followed east for 12.7 miles to Yellow Creek Gap.

Initial location and marking of the Trail in this area was completed in 1932–33 by the Smoky Mountains Hiking Club.

After 1946, Fontana Dam and the development of Fontana Village, with its opportunities as a recreational and mountain-climbing center, made crossing the Little Tennessee River at Fontana Dam feasible.

From Fontana Dam, for about one mile, the route now follows a hard-surfaced highway toward N.C. 28, then it picks up a ridgecrest path through woods to Fontana Boat Dock parking area. In 1971, the USFS relocated the A.T. from the boat dock parking area at N.C. 28 to ascend to Walker Gap on Yellow Creek Mountain *via* Bee Cove Lead. This is an elevation change of 1,650 feet in 2.5 miles. The Trail then heads east along Yellow Creek Mountain to rejoin the former Trail route at Black Gum Gap.

Points of Interest

Fontana Dam, part of the TVA system, was constructed on the Little Tennessee River during and after World War II to furnish hydroelectric power. The dam is 480 feet high, the highest in eastern America. The powerhouse and penstock are at the bottom near the center of the river channel. The dam impounded the Little Tennessee River for 29 miles to create Fontana Lake, making the southern boundary of the Great Smoky Mountains National Park a water boundary.

In May 1946, Fontana Village was constructed at Welch Cove to house TVA construction workers. It now serves as a recreation area and resort. The village is two miles from the dam at an elevation of 1,800 feet, immediately at the base of the Yellow Creek Mountains. Extensive facilities are available, including a lodge, restaurants, drugstore, grocery store, post office, and laundry. About 300 houses, which were used in the original construction, are now available for guests. The village has an extensive recreation program that features hiking, fishing, and horseback riding.

The dam, which created the lake with a shoreline elevation of about 1,710 feet, flooded out N.C. 288 from Deals Gap to Bryson City. Hard-surfaced N.C. 28 leads from U.S. 129 to Fontana Dam (9.5 miles from Deals Gap) and continues to a junction with U.S. 19 about nine miles south of Bryson City.

Farther down the Little Tennessee River is Cheoah Dam, which is just above the bridge used by the former A.T. route. The dam is 200 feet high and backs up the river for six miles. Below is Calderwood Lake, made by the Calderwood Dam, located farther down river.

Road Approaches

The northern end of this section crosses N.C. 28 about 1.8 miles from Fontana Dam and about two miles east of Fontana Village.

In Yellow Creek Gap, the Trail crosses Yellow Creek Mountain Road 8.2 miles south of Fontana Dam. Four miles east of this crossing is N.C. 28. About ten miles to the west is U.S. 129.

Bus service is not available to Fontana; you may wish to call ATC to inquire about shuttles, (304) 535-6331, or use the shuttle at Fontana boat dock.

Maps

See ATC's Nantahala National Forest map with this guide and TVA Fontana Dam quadrangle. For map of Fontana Village, ask for location map from Fontana Village, Fontana Dam, NC 28733.

Shelters, Campsites, and Water

Fontana Dam Shelter is located in the TVA complex at Fontana Dam. Cable Gap Shelter is 7.3 miles from the northern end of the section. Both shelters have reliable water sources.

Water sources are infrequent, and even well-recognized sources may fail in dry seasons. Make ample provisions for water.

Public Accommodations and Services

Fontana Village, two miles west of the A.T. on N.C. 28, is an excellent supply source, with a general store, hostel, cabins, restaurants, and post office.

Trail Description, North to South

Miles	Data
0.0	From the northern bank of the Little Tennessee River, follow the roadway across the dam.
0.4	Reach the southern bank. On the right at the southern abutment of dam are visitors' buildings with exhibits, a refreshment stand (closed in winter), restrooms, and public showers. Ascend on hard-surfaced road.
0.7	At ridgecrest, pass parking overlook on left, with good views of Fontana Lake, its dam and powerhouse to the Great Smokies and a picnic area with water fountains, restrooms (closed in winter), and, 300 feet into the woods, the **Fontana Dam Shelter**. Descend on hard-surfaced road.
0.9	Bear left onto Trail into woods, continuing along curving ridgecrest, with gentle ascents and descents.
1.7	Descend to hard-surfaced road (N.C. 1245) at swimming pool, bear left, and cross road. At the top of rise pass through hard-surfaced road and parking area (bulletin board). Road drops steeply to boat docks; bear right around concrete comfort stations (closed in winter), and ascend on grassy slope and stone steps to N.C. 28.
1.8	Reach N.C. 28, parking available on the right at the intersection. Fontana Village is two miles to the right. Cross

road, and ascend stone steps. Ascend gradually along narrow ridgecrest.

2.1   Bear right at head of draw, then turn sharply right.

2.5   Water is to the right, immediately below Trail.

3.0   Pass through gap, and turn sharply right along Bee Cove Lead. Ascend along right side of ridgecrest.

3.4   Take sharply left.

3.5   Pass rock cliffs on the right.

3.6   Regain crest of Bee Cove Lead, and turn sharply right, ascending steeply along crest.

4.0   Trail bears right from Bee Cove Lead.

4.2   Trail crosses stream.

4.3   Trail crosses another stream and bears left.

4.5   Reach Walker Gap at 3,450 feet on the crest of Yellow Creek Mountain. Note trail intersection: Fontana Village is 2.7 miles *via* Yellow Creek Mountain and Lookout Rock trails. Turn left along A.T.

5.1   Cross high point, with rocks on summit, at 3,720 feet.

5.2   Cross another high point, descend, and continue along crest, ascending and descending.

5.9   Pass through Black Gum Gap.

6.2   With High Top (highest point on Yellow Creek Mountain, 3,786 feet) ahead, leave ridgecrest, and skirt the right side.

6.5   Bear south to switchback, then bear left along southern slope, descending toward Cable Gap with Cable Gap Shelter visible ahead. Descend with views to the south.

7.1   Turn sharply right, downhill.

7.3   Turn sharply left. **Cable Gap Shelter** on right. (Built in 1939 by the CCC, under the direction of the Nantahala National Forest; refurbished in 1988 by the Smoky Mountains Hiking Club.) A privy is close by, and a spring is adjacent to the shelter. From the shelter, ascend southern slope of Tommy Knob.

8.2   Reach road intersection in Yellow Creek Gap at 2,980 feet. To left, it is four miles to N.C. 28, where several motels are near the intersection. Fontana Village is nine miles farther to left on N.C. 28, a total of 13 miles from Yellow Creek Gap. The A.T. continues directly opposite, up stone steps into woods.

Trail Description, South to North

Miles   **Data**

0.0   From road in Yellow Creek Gap (2,980 feet), proceed along
        left side of ridge. It is four miles to N.C. 28, where several
        motels are near the intersection. Fontana Village is nine
        miles farther to left on N.C. 28, a total of 13 miles from
        Yellow Creek Gap.

0.5   Start descent into Cable Gap.

0.9   Pass **Cable Gap Shelter** on left. Shelter, with adjacent
        spring, was built in 1939 by the CCC for the Nantahala
        National Forest; refurbished in 1988 by Smoky Mountains
        Hiking Club. A privy is close to the shelter.

1.1   Turn sharply left, climbing southern side of High Top
        (3,786 feet), the highest point on the Yellow Creek Range.
        Dense growth precludes many views. Ascend the south-
        ern slope, from which Yellow Creek Valley can be seen.

1.7   Switch back, and bear north along a spur of High Top.

2.0   Reach the ridgecrest, where Fontana Lake can be observed
        to the right. Continue west along the main crest.

2.3   Pass through Black Gum Gap, and continue along crest,
        ascending and descending.

2.9   Cross high point of ridgecrest.

3.1   Cross another high point, with rocks on summit, at 3,720
        feet.

3.7   Reach Walker Gap at 3,450 feet. Note trail intersection:
        Fontana Village is 2.7 miles straight ahead *via* the Yellow
        Creek Mountain and Lookout Rock trails. Turn right on
        the A.T., and descend.

3.9   Trail bears right.

4.0   Cross small stream.

4.1   Cross a larger stream.

4.2   Trail bears left along ridgecrest of Bee Cove Lead.

4.5   Descend steeply.

4.6   Trail turns sharply to left.

4.7   Pass rock cliffs on the left, and turn right.

5.1   Pass through gap, and turn sharply left, leaving Bee Cove
        Lead.

5.6   Water is on the left, immediately below Trail.

6.0   Reach ridgecrest, and bear left.

6.4   Reach N.C. 28. Fontana Village is two miles to left. Cross road, immediately descend stone steps, and turn right down grassy slope. Pass a concrete comfort station on the right (closed in winter), and reach hard-surfaced N.C. 1245; parking available. Turn left along road toward swimming pool, and enter woods to right. Ascend to ridgecrest, and follow Trail, ascending and descending gently.

7.1   Reach hard-surfaced road, and continue toward Fontana Dam.

7.5   Pass picnic area and trail to **Fontana Dam Shelter** on the right, and descend along road to the dam.

7.8   Reach the southern end of the dam. On left are visitors' buildings with exhibits, refreshment stand (closed in winter), restrooms, and public showers. Cross dam on road.

8.2   Reach the northern bank of the Little Tennessee River and end of section. A.T. continues right on lakeshore road. (See Section Two.)

Yellow Creek Gap to Stecoah Gap
Section Four
7.6 miles

Brief Description of Section

The A.T. crosses Yellow Creek Mountain Road at the crest of
Yellow Creek Gap (2,980 feet). Stone steps lead into the woods.
From here, the A.T. begins a long ascent to Cody Gap, runs a similar
distance along the crest, and then takes a steep descent to Brown
Fork Gap. The Trail resumes a steep ascent, levels off slightly, and
begins a long descent to Sweetwater Gap. Another up-and-down
climb brings the hiker to Stecoah Gap.

Points of Interest

Excellent views of Cheoah Bald and a side trail to Wauchecha
Bald highlight this section. The Trail formerly went to the summit
of Wauchecha (4,385 feet), but that route is now part of a loop trail
of less than one mile.

Road Approaches

In Yellow Creek Gap, the A.T. crosses the Yellow Creek Mountain Road (hard-surfaced N.C. 1242) 8.2 miles south of Fontana
Dam. Four miles east of this crossing is N.C. 28. To the west, U.S. 129
is about 10 miles.

In Stecoah Gap, 13.6 miles north of Wesser, the Trail crosses N.C.
143 (Sweetwater Creek Road); parking available. N.C. 28 is about
three miles to the east, and Robbinsville is 8.6 miles to the west.

Maps

TVA Fontana Dam and Hewitt quadrangles; ATC Nantahala
National Forest map with this guide.

Shelters, Campsites, and Water

Brown Fork Gap Shelter is located 5.2 miles from the northern end of the section. This shelter was constructed in 1997 by volunteers from Smoky Mountain Hiking Club, ATC's Konnarock volunteer crew, and the U.S. Forest Service. Water is usually available near Cody Gap, Brown Fork Gap, and Stecoah Gap, but, in dry seasons, those water sources may be unreliable.

Public Accommodations and Services

From Stecoah Gap, it is 10 miles west on a hard-surfaced road (N.C. 143) to Robbinsville, which has public accommodations and services, including grocery stores, restaurant, and post office.

Trail Description, North to South

Miles	Data
0.0	From road intersection at the crest of Yellow Creek Gap (2,980 feet), ascend stone steps, and enter woods on Trail. Bear to right of ridgecrest, ascending.
0.4	Cross stream at foot of small cascade.
1.4	Reach main ridgecrest, and bear right.
1.6	Cross knob, with view of Cheoah Bald to left.
1.7	Bear right from ridgecrest.
2.4	Regain ridgecrest, and bear right along crest. Reach Cody Gap. Bear left on Trail, out of gap. Continue on Trail, with little elevation change, around side of ridge.
3.2	Pass through Hogback Gap, and ascend to knob at 3,912 feet. Turn left (east) along ridgecrest, and descend.
5.0	Pass through Brown Fork Gap. Ascend slightly.
5.1	Enter gap. Water usually can be found 35 yards to the left. Ascend slightly.
5.2	Reach junction, with trail on left leading about 70 yards to **Brown Fork Gap Shelter**, with adjacent spring. Privy is below shelter.
5.6	Reach narrow ridgecrest, which Trail follows, descending in southerly course.

5.8   Pass cliffs, 15 yards to right, with views of Snowbird Mountains. Descend steeply.
6.6   Pass through Sweetwater Gap. Ascend.
6.8   Reach ridgecrest, and descend gradually.
7.6   Reach N.C. 143 in Stecoah Gap at 3,165 feet; parking available. About 10 miles downhill to the right, accommodations are available in Robbinsville.

Trail Description, South to North

Miles   **Data**

0.0   Cross N.C. 143 in Stecoah Gap (3,165 feet), and ascend to ridgecrest; parking available. About 10 miles downhill to the left, accommodations are available in Robbinsville.
0.8   Reach the top of ridge, and descend steeply to Sweetwater Gap.
1.0   Pass through Sweetwater Gap, and ascend steeply to rock cliffs.
1.8   Reach cliffs, 15 yards to left, with excellent views of Snowbird Mountains.
2.0   Reach crest of narrow ridge, then gradually descend into gap.
2.4   Reach side trail to right about 70 yards to **Brown Fork Gap Shelter**, with adjacent spring. Privy is located below shelter. Ascend slightly.
2.5   Pass through gap; water usually can be found 35 yards to the right. Ascend knob.
2.6   Trail passes through Brown Fork Gap and makes a series of small ascents and descents.
3.3   Reach the crest of knob (3,912 feet). Descend into Hogback Gap.
4.4   In Hogback Gap, bear right on Trail. Continue, with little elevation change, around the side of ridge.
5.2   Enter Cody Gap, and bear right along the ridgecrest.
5.6   Bear left, away from crest.
5.9   Rejoin ridgecrest, and bear left along crest.
6.0   Cross knob with excellent view of Cheoah Bald to right.
6.2   Bear left away from ridgecrest.

7.2 Cross stream at foot of small cascade, and descend into Yellow Creek Gap.

7.6 Reach Yellow Creek Gap (2,980 feet). Hard-surfaced road to the right leads to N.C. 28, where several motels are near the intersection. Fontana Village is about 13 miles from the gap along this road and N.C. 28. The A.T. continues directly opposite, across the road.

Stecoah Gap to the Nantahala River
(Wesser, North Carolina)
Section Five
13.6 Miles

Brief Description of Section

This section of the A.T. involves the steep ascent and descent of Cheoah Bald (5,062 feet). Switchbacks and small knobs along the crests are prevalent. The A.T. crosses the Nantahala River at the southern end of this section, in the middle of the Nantahala Outdoor Center in Wesser.

Points of Interest

At the summit of Cheoah Bald, a short side trail leads to a lookout point. The views from Cheoah are among the best in the southern Appalachians. Also worth noting are the rock formations of Nantahala slate that form a knife edge south of the Cheoah summit. Farther south, the route offers good views of the Nantahala Gorge and passes through a beautiful hardwood cove on its descent to Wesser.

Road Approaches

On the northern end, the A.T. crosses N.C. 143 at Stecoah Gap. N.C. 28 is about three miles to the east, and Robbinsville is 10 miles to the west.

The southern end is at U.S. 19 in Wesser. Bryson City is 15 miles northeast on U.S. 19; Murphy is 38 miles south.

Maps

TVA Hewitt and Wesser and quadrangles, and ATC Nantahala National Forest map.

Shelters, Campsites, and Water

The Sassafras Gap Shelter is located almost midway along this section, about 120 yards off the A.T. The A. Rufus Morgan Shelter is 0.8 mile south of Wesser, in Section Six. While this section usually has many fine springs and water sources, hikers are encouraged to carry water during dry seasons.

Public Accommodations and Services

Wesser has lodging, restaurants, and a store. The Nantahala Outdoor Center (Wesser) is an excellent supply point and has a hostel, and packages may be mailed there (Nantahala Outdoor Center, 13077 Highway 19W, Bryson City, NC 28713). From Wesser, it is 15 miles northeast to Bryson City on U.S. 19. From Stecoah Gap, it is 10 miles to Robbinsville, with public accommodations.

Trail Description, North to South

Miles	Data
0.0	From road at crest of Stecoah Gap (3,165 feet; parking available), follow Trail up steps to left of ridgecrest, gradually ascending south through a series of switchbacks.
0.7	Reach high point of ridge, turn right, and pass over a series of small knobs along crest. At crest, a good spring is about 0.1 mile to the right on logging road.
2.1	Pass through Simp Gap. Ascend, and follow Trail over a series of small knobs.
3.1	Pass through Locust Cove Gap. Water is located 150 yards to the right; spring is variable. Follow Trail to right, leading out of gap, ascending gradually to ridgecrest.
3.4	Reach ridgecrest, and turn sharply to the left.
5.1	Yellow-blazed Bartram Trail joins A.T. from the right.
5.5	Reach the summit of Cheoah Bald (5,062 feet), with fantastic views at terminus of the Bartram Trail. Trail to left leads to lookout point. From the summit, descend south along knife edge of blue Nantahala slate.

5.6   Bear to the right of the ridgecrest, and descend gradually into Sassafras Gap.

6.7   Pass through Sassafras Gap. **Sassafras Gap Shelter** is approximately 120 yards on trail to right; spring is behind the shelter. From the gap, ascend along the northern side of knob, then descend.

7.0   Cross gap, and ascend toward summit of Swim Bald.

7.6   Reach summit of Swim Bald (4,720 feet). *Care should be exercised at this point.* Bear somewhat to the south, and go onto main ridge. Another ridge extends from Swim Bald down to the northern end and is often confused with the one running almost directly east. An unreliable spring is approximately 50 yards east of the summit of Swim Bald on left. Along the ridge that the A.T. follows are good views of the Nantahala Gorge. This ridge becomes exceedingly sharp, especially on the southern slope.

8.3   Trail turns very sharply to the left and gently descends into a beautiful hardwood cove.

8.8   Trail switches back sharply to the right and descends gradually into gap, passing a reliable spring at the Jumpup.

9.3   Enter gap, and continue along ridgecrest.

9.6   Reach ridgecrest, and descend along side of ridge.

10.5   Reach Grassy Gap (3,050 feet). Bear right along heavily used Trail around side of Tyre Knob.

10.6   Pass through sag. Trail to right leads about 100 yards to spring.

10.7   Reach ridgecrest running south from Tyre Knob campsite (3,760 feet). Bear right, descending along ridgecrest.

12.0   Reach dirt road at Wright Gap. Cross road, and ascend to ridgecrest.

12.3   Cross under powerline, and follow Trail along side of Flint Ridge.

13.4   Reach ridge spur, and descend gradually to railroad tracks.

13.5   Reach railroad tracks, cross tracks, and continue straight through parking lot to footbridge across the Nantahala River. Cross bridge.

13.6   Reach eastern bank of Nantahala River in the center of NOC facilities in Wesser (1,723 feet). To continue on A.T., cross U.S. 19, then cross small paved road, and ascend graded trail into woods. *Note:* This description covers a short relocation expected to be completed in 1998 or 1999. Look for blazes at railroad and on U.S. 19.

Trail Description, South to North

Miles   **Data**

0.0   At U.S. 19 in Wesser (1,723 feet) along eastern bank of Nantahala River, cross highway and footbridge, continue straight across parking lot to railroad tracks. Note: A short relocation was expected to be completed in 1998 or 1999. Look for, and follow, blazes.

0.1   Leave railroad tracks, and take Trail to right, gradually ascending to ridge spur.

0.7   Reach crest of ridge spur, and follow Trail along side of Flint Ridge.

1.3   Cross under powerline.

1.6   Descend to dirt road at Wright Gap. Cross road, and make steep ascent of ridge to Tyre Top.

2.3   Near the base of Tyre Top, proceed left to skirt the southeast side of Tyre Top (3,760 feet).

2.5   Descend into sag. The trail to left leads about 100 yards to a **campsite** with a spring.

3.1   Reach Grassy Gap (3,050 feet), ascend, and skirt eastern side of ridge.

3.5   Reach crest of Grassy Top, and descend into gap.

4.8   From gap, Trail turns to right and gradually ascends into a beautiful hardwood cove, passing a reliable spring.

5.3   Trail switches back sharply to the left and gradually ascends to knife edge of rock.

6.0   Reach summit of Swim Bald, bear slightly to the right, and descend. On the opposite side is a splendid view of the Smokies. Unreliable spring is about 50 yards to the right. It lies in a grassy notch, where the eastern ridge (A.T.) from Swim Bald and the northern ridge converge.

6.6   Cross gap, and proceed along right side of knob.

6.9   Descend into Sassafras Gap. **Sassafras Gap Shelter** is about 120 yards on the trail to left. A spring is located behind the shelter. From this gap, climb toward Cheoah Bald. Ascent is steep at first, then gradual.

8.0   Reach crest, turn sharply right uphill, and ascend along knife edge of blue Nantahala slate.

8.1   Reach the summit of Cheoah Bald (5,062 feet). This peak offers one of the most splendid panoramas in the southern Appalachians. Trail to the right leads to lookout point for striking view of the Great Smokies. A.T. bears left. Descent is gradual.

8.5   Turn sharply right from the descending ridge.

9.8   Reach old A.T. junction. Follow Trail to left, gradually descending around the side and over the ridge spur into Locust Cove Gap.

10.5 Pass through Locust Cove Gap. Path to left leads about 150 yards to a variable spring. Trail leads to the left out of the gap, switching back to ridgecrest.

10.7 Return to ridgecrest, and follow Trail over a series of small knobs.

11.5 Pass through Simp Gap, and ascend to high point of ridge.

12.9 Reach highest point of the ridge. Turn sharply to the left. *Exercise caution here.* Follow Trail on gradual descent through a series of switchbacks to Stecoah Gap.

13.6 Reach Stecoah Gap (3,165 feet), on top of divide; parking available on right side of A.T. Robbinsville is located 10 miles to left on hard-surfaced N.C. 143; accommodations and supplies are available there.

Nantahala River
(Wesser, North Carolina)
to Tellico Gap
Section Six
7.9 Miles

Brief Description of Section

This section begins in the middle of the Nantahala Outdoor Center at Wesser on U.S. 19. The Trail climbs steeply from Wesser (1,723 feet) over Wesser Bald (4,627 feet) and then descends to Tellico Gap (3,850 feet).

Points of Interest

Near the middle of the section is the "Jumpup," with extensive views of Cheoah Bald to the west, the Smokies to the north, and the Balsam Mountains to the east. At Wesser Bald, a lookout tower provides a superb view of ranges in all directions.

Road Approaches

Wesser is on U.S. 19, 15 miles southwest of Bryson City and 38 miles north of Murphy. Tellico Gap, at the southern end of the section, can be reached from the west by gravel N.C. 1365 (Otter Creek Road), four miles from paved N.C. 1310, and from the east, eight miles *via* Tellico Road from N.C. 28, 12 miles north of Franklin.

Shelters, Campsites, and Water

The A. Rufus Morgan Shelter, named for the NHC's founder, is 0.8 mile south of Wesser and 7.1 miles north of Tellico Gap. Water for the shelter is available from the stream across the A.T. from the shelter.

Wesser Bald Shelter, 5.7 miles south of Wesser, and 2.1 miles north of Tellico Gap, was built by the Nantahala Hiking Club in 1994. A campsite is located near the shelter, and water for both is available from the spring 0.1 mile south on the Trail.

Water is scarce in this section, and the only reliable sources are the two described above. There is no water in Tellico Gap.

Maps

USFS map of the Nantahala National Forest and the TVA Wesser quadrangle. (Relocations of the A.T. are not shown on those maps. See ATC Nantahala National Forest map with this guide.)

Public Accommodations and Services

Wesser has a hostel and motel, restaurants, store, and other facilities. The Nantahala Outdoor Center adjacent to the Trail is an excellent supply point, and packages may be mailed there (Nantahala Outdoor Center, 13077 Highway 19W, Bryson City, NC 28713). From Wesser, it is 15 miles northeast to Bryson City on U.S. 19.

Trail Description, North to South

Miles   Data

0.0   Section begins on U.S. 19 in Wesser (1,723 feet) near motel office. Cross small paved road, and ascend graded trail into woods. NOTE: This route depended on completion (expected in 1998) of short relocation near NOC. Follow the blazes!

0.8   Enter clearing. **A. Rufus Morgan Shelter** is 200 feet to left, and a stream is on right.

1.1   At gap, turn right on old road in small clearing. Follow road for 600 feet, then turn left into woods.

3.9   Begin rock-and-wood steps. Pass small cave to right.

4.1   Reach "Jumpup," a rocky outcrop boasting outstanding views. Trail follows ridge with many short ups and downs.

5.7   Blue-blazed Wesser Creek Trail (old A.T.) intersects from left. To right on side trail is **Wesser Bald Shelter**.

5.8   Trail turns sharply right. Blue-blazed trail ahead leads 125 feet to excellent spring.

6.5   Reach high point near Wesser Bald summit (4,627 feet). A.T. bears right and descends. Trail straight ahead leads 120 feet to former firetower, with magnificent views.

7.9   Reach Tellico Gap. Gravel road on right leads four miles to N.C. 1310. Tellico Bald goes left eight miles to N.C. 28. Rough road going uphill on left leads to firetower. A.T. crosses road in gap (3,850 feet) as it climbs under powerline.

Trail Description, South to North

Miles   **Data**

0.0   A.T. bears left, leaves Tellico Gap (3,850 feet) on graded trail to left of gravel road (parking available) to firetower, and begins climb to Wesser Bald.

1.4   Reach top of climb on rocky ledge near Wesser Bald summit (4,627 feet). Trail to right leads 120 feet to firetower; magnificent views. A.T. bears left and begins descent.

2.1   Trail makes sharp left turn. Trail on right leads 125 feet to excellent spring.

2.2   Reach trails junction; to left, short trail leads to **Wesser Bald Shelter**. To right is blue-blazed Wesser Creek Trail (former A.T.). A.T. continues ahead, up ridge, with many short ups and downs for next two miles.

3.8   Reach "Jumpup," a rocky outcrop with outstanding view. Trail turns sharply right and descends steeply.

6.8   Trail makes right turn onto old road. Follow road for 600 feet, then turn left on sidehill trail.

7.1   Enter clearing. **A. Rufus Morgan Shelter** is 200 feet to right in small cove. Water from stream is available on left.

7.9   Turn sharply left down graded trail to small, paved road just behind hostel office on U.S. 19 at Wesser (1,723 feet). To continue on Trail, go across highway and take foot-bridge across river into NOC. Note: This route includes a short 1998-1999 relocation. Follow blazes!

Tellico Gap to Wayah Gap
Section Seven
13.5 Miles

Brief Description of Section

This section follows the main ridge of the Nantahala Mountains, going near the tops of seven balds above 5,000 feet. The Trail is graded throughout, with a few steep places, and avoids the summits of peaks without views and of Wine Spring Bald, which has multiple radio and television installations.

Points of Interest

The observation tower on the summit of Wayah Bald (5,342 feet) has extensive views of the surrounding mountains, from Georgia to the Great Smokies.

A 0.1-mile side trail is open to Wilson Lick, site of an early ranger station in the Nantahala Forest. Another 0.2-mile side trail leads to fine views from the summit of Rocky Bald.

Road Approaches

Tellico Gap, the northern end of the section, is accessible *via* a four-mile gravel N.C. 1365 and Otter Creek Road, with Tellico Gap sign from N.C. 1310, which links U.S. 19 south of Wesser and U.S. 64 west of Franklin and also crosses the A.T. at Wayah Gap, the southern end of the section. N.C. 1365 (Tellico Road on this side) is also passable to the east, eight miles to N.C. 28, between Franklin and Bryson City, North Carolina. Another gravel road (N.C. 1397), reached from N.C. 1310 at a sign for Burningtown Gap, provides access to the A.T. at Burningtown Gap near the middle of the section. (Burningtown Gap is not accessible from the east.) The A.T. at the summit of Wayah Bald can be reached from Wayah Gap by USFS 69, which roughly parallels the southern half of this section to the west. N.C. 1310 crosses the A.T. in Wayah Gap. From Wayah Gap, it is seven miles east to U.S. 64 and 12 miles east, on N.C. 1310 and U.S. 64 to Franklin.

Maps

USFS map of the Nantahala National Forest and the TVA Wayah Bald and Wesser quadrangles. Relocations are not shown on those maps; see ATC Nantahala National Forest map with this guide.

Shelters, Campsites, and Water

This section has one shelter with a good campsite. The Cold Spring Shelter is 3.6 miles south of Tellico Gap. This very old shelter still has remnants of the fencing that kept cattle and hogs from the shelter.

A campsite is located on the ridge just above the shelter that is reached by a side trail just north of the shelter.

Water is available at the shelter and at four springs referenced in Trail descriptions. Water may also be obtained at Licklog Gap by going west about half a mile downhill to a stream.

The area that has been developed around the observation tower on Wayah Bald is off-limits to camping. Wayah Bald has no water.

Water is not available at either end of this section.

Public Accommodations

This section has no public accommodations or supply sources at either end.

Trail Description, North to South

Miles	Data
0.0	A.T. is a graded trail that crosses Tellico Gap (3,850 feet) under a powerline.
1.4	Reach a good spring on right, after a long climb.
1.7	Blue-blazed side trail to left leads 0.2 mile to nice viewpoint on summit of Rocky Bald. The grade on A.T. is

moderate as Trail slabs the western sides of Rocky, Black, and Tellico balds and returns to ridge between them.

2.9   Reach vista just left of Trail. Trail leaves ridge and goes around western side of Copper Ridge Bald, then starts descent.

3.6   Reach **Cold Spring Shelter** and spring. A **campsite** is located on ridge above shelter.

4.8   Reach Burningtown Gap (4,236 feet), a large clearing with apple trees. Dirt N.C. 1397 is to right, leading to N.C. 1310 at Kyle. A.T. is graded trail crossing the area and bearing right to woods.

5.6   Reach small clearing where several grassed roads intersect. A.T. is graded trail ascending from clearing.

7.1   Reach Licklog Gap with a logging road and wildlife clearing a short distance to the west.

8.8   A.T. makes right turn, and yellow-blazed Bartram Trail comes in here and follows the A.T. for the next 2.4 miles.

8.9   Reach sloping spring to right of Trail.

9.1   Cross dirt road.

9.3   Reach summit of Wayah Bald (5,342 feet) and stone observation tower. Leave tower area *via* macadam path.

9.4   A.T. and Bartram Trail bear right into woods just past latrines and just before parking area.

9.6   Descend log steps, and cross woods road.

11.0   Trail bears right onto woods road.

11.2   Reach Wine Spring on right. In 100 feet, Bartram Trail turns right, and A.T. bears left.

11.7   Descend log steps, and cross gravel USFS 69. A piped spring is located a few feet to left.

12.2   Reach side trail to historic Wilson Lick ranger station on right.

13.5   One hundred feet east of crest of Wayah Gap, reach paved N.C. 1310 (4,180 feet), across from picnic area (latrines and trash cans). To continue on A.T., cross road, and climb log steps.

Trail Description, South to North

Miles	Data

Miles   **Data**

0.0   A.T. crosses N.C. 1310 in Wayah Gap (4,180 feet) and climbs in woods. Trail parallels USFS 69 from gap for one mile.

1.3   Reach junction with blue-blazed trail to historic Wilson Lick ranger station on left.

1.8   Cross gravel USFS 69. Piped spring is several feet to the right of crossing.

2.3   Reach junction with Bartram Trail, marked with yellow blazes, which joins on the left. In 100 feet, reach Wine Spring, just left of Trail.

2.5   Trail bears left off old road, which continues to Wine Spring Road.

3.9   Cross woods road, and ascend log steps.

4.1   Bear left onto macadam path leading to Wayah Bald.

4.2   Reach stone observation tower on summit of Wayah Bald (5,342 feet), with extensive views. Trail leaves tower area opposite path entrance.

4.4   Cross woods road.

4.6   Spring is located to the left of the Trail.

4.7   A.T. makes left turn, and Bartram Trail (yellow blazes) makes right turn. Trail soon reaches nearly level ridge.

6.4   Reach Licklog Gap. A logging road and wildlife clearing are visible to left.

7.9   Enter small clearing at junction of several grassy roads. Trail continues into woods.

8.7   After crossing two small streams, reach Burningtown Gap (4,236 feet), a large clearing with apple trees. Dirt N.C. 1397 is to the left. Trail crosses field and starts climb toward Burningtown Bald by graded trail.

9.9   Reach **Cold Spring Shelter** and spring to the right on Trail. **Campsites** are on ridge above shelter.

10.6   After slabbing western side of Copper Ridge Bald (5,200 feet), reach vista just right of Trail. Nice views of Little

Tennessee River Valley. Trail continues along ridge, skirting western sides of Tellico, Black, and Rocky balds.

11.8   Side trail to right leads to Rocky Bald lookout.

12.1   Pass good spring on left. Trail descends steadily from here.

13.5   Reach Tellico Gap (3,850 feet), just after passing under powerline. Gravel N.C. 1365 leads left four miles to N.C. 1310 and right eight miles to N.C. 28. Rough road ascending ahead leads to firetower. A.T. bears left between the two roads.

Wayah Gap to Wallace Gap
Section Eight
9.0 Miles

Brief Description of Section

This section begins in Wayah Gap (4,180 feet), climbs to a shoulder of Siler Bald (5,216 feet), crosses a series of knobs and gaps and a major highway (U.S. 64) in Winding Stair Gap (3,850 feet), then returns to a level ridge until descending into Wallace Gap (3,738 feet).

Points of Interest

The highest point on this section is Siler Bald (5,216 feet), named for William Siler, whose great-grandson, the Reverend A. Rufus Morgan, helped establish the A.T. in North Carolina. This bald has been cleared and is maintained as a grassy bald by the USFS. The views include the route of the A.T. from Tray Mountain in Georgia to the Great Smokies and are well worth the 0.2-mile side trip.

Road Approaches

U.S. 64, which crosses the Trail at Winding Stair Gap, is a major access point for the Trail. Franklin is 10 miles east. However, several hikers' cars were vandalized while parked overnight here in the early 1990s.

Wayah Gap can be reached by N.C. 1310, seven miles west of U.S. 64 and 12 miles west of Franklin. Wallace Gap is on "Old 64" and USFS 67, but Rock Gap, with parking, (see next section) is a better Trailhead.

Maps

TVA Wayah Bald and Rainbow Springs quadrangles. Relocations of the A.T. are not shown on those maps; see ATC Nantahala National Forest map with this guide.

Shelters, Campsites, and Water

Siler Bald Shelter is located about halfway along the section on a 1.1-mile blue-blazed loop trail. The northern junction with the A.T. is 1.7 miles south of Wayah Gap. A spring is located 300 feet south of the shelter on the loop trail. Another spring is located at the Trailhead in Winding Stair Gap.

Trash cans are located at Winding Stair Gap and in the Wayah Crest picnic area near the Trail at Wayah Gap.

Public Accommodations and Services

Franklin, located 10 miles east of Winding Stair Gap *via* U.S. 64, has motels, restaurants, post office, groceries, outdoor equipment, and a hospital.

USFS Standing Indian Campground has a public telephone and is located 1.5 miles south of Wallace Gap on paved USFS 67.

Rainbow Springs Campground, a commercial campground with showers, bunkroom, and small store, is 1.1 miles west of Wallace Gap on "Old 64."

Trail Description, North to South

Miles	Data
0.0	One hundred feet east of ridgecrest of Wayah Gap, Trail crosses N.C. 1310 (4,180 feet). Skirt Wayah Crest picnic area (latrines and trash cans available), cross dirt road, and ascend by graded trail.
1.7	Reach grassy wildlife clearing. To right, open summit of Siler Bald (5,216 feet) is 0.2 mile, with spectacular views. To left, blue-blazed **Siler Bald Shelter** Loop Trail descends 0.6 mile on logging roads to shelter. A.T. continues straight into woods.
2.0	Trail bends right and crosses old, overgrown road.
2.1	Make sharp left turn onto woods road at log steps.
2.2	Reach southern end of **Siler Bald Shelter** Loop Trail. A.T. bears right, downhill. Blue-blazed trail loops north 0.5 mile to shelter.

3.9   Reach Panther Gap, a level area with **campsites** but no water.
4.8   Turn sharply left at Swinging Lick Gap.
4.9   Cross stream.
5.6   Cross stream.
5.9   Reach Winding Stair Gap after crossing stream on bridge by waterfall. A.T. climbs bank to reach U.S. 64 and turns right for 500 feet to parking area. Southbound A.T. goes left up steps just beyond parking area. A piped spring is beside the steps leading south.
6.6   Cross stream.
7.6   Reach ridge at gap with eastern view. Trail becomes level.
8.4   Descend log steps to small clearing.
8.9   Cross stream, and bear right down long row of log steps.
9.0   Reach Wallace Gap (3,738 feet). A.T. crosses "Old 64" on left of road leading 1.5 miles to **Standing Indian Campground**.

Trail Description, South to North

Miles   **Data**

0.0   In Wallace Gap (3,738 feet), A.T. crosses "Old 64" and climbs road bank opposite paved road leading 1.5 miles to **Standing Indian Campground**.
0.1   After long flight of log steps, cross stream.
0.6   Reach small, level area. Trail continues up log steps to level path along ridge.
2.4   Cross stream.
3.1   Reach Winding Stair Gap, with parking area, piped spring, and U.S. 64. Trail turns right, follows highway for 500 feet, then crosses and descends bank into woods. One hundred feet farther, cross gravel road and bridge across small stream, just below waterfall.
3.4   Cross stream.
4.1   Cross stream.
4.2   Reach Swinging Lick Gap. Trail makes sharp right and continues ascent.
5.1   Reach Panther Gap.

6.8 Reach southern end of **Siler Bald Shelter** Loop Trail. Blue-blazed trail behind and to right loops 0.5 mile to shelter and spring. A.T. bears left and continues on woods road for 250 feet, then turns sharply right uphill.

7.3 Reach northern end of **Siler Bald Shelter** Loop Trail in clearing. A.T. continues straight across clearing. To left, it is 0.2 mile to summit of Siler Bald, with magnificent views. Shelter is 0.6 mile to right on blue-blazed loop trail.

9.0 Cross woods road, skirt Wayah Crest picnic area and picnic area (latrines and trash cans), and reach paved N.C. 1310 in Wayah Gap (4,180 feet). Trail continues across road.

Wallace Gap to Deep Gap
Section Nine
21.3 Miles

Brief Description of Section

In this section, the Trail completes its traverse of the Nantahala Range and reaches the Blue Ridge at Ridgepole Mountain. It turns west, then northwest, with the ridges, making a long sweep around the headwaters of the Nantahala River and Standing Indian Campground.

With the notable exception of the steep section just south of Albert Mountain, changes in elevation are gradual and afford pleasant hiking. The seven access trails to the A.T. from USFS 67 and Standing Indian Campground make this section popular for loop hikes, and it is often full of hikers.

Points of Interest

Standing Indian Mountain (5,498 feet) is the highest point on the Trail south of the Great Smokies. The views to the south and west reveal the ranges the Trail follows southward and provide ample reward for the 0.1-mile side trip to the summit.

Albert Mountain boasts one of the few remaining fire towers and offers superb views of the Blue Ridge to the east and of the Little Tennessee River Valley below. At Albert, the Trail follows the western boundary of Coweeta Hydrologic Laboratory, famous for its 50-plus years of research into tree-water relationships.

From Mooney Gap to Deep Gap, 13.1 miles, the Trail is within the Southern Nantahala Wilderness Area.

Road Approaches

To reach Wallace Gap, follow U.S. 64 12 miles west from Franklin, then turn left at sign for "Appalachian Trail and Standing Indian Campground." Follow "Old 64" for about two miles. Wallace Gap is on this road, but it is not a good place to park. Rock Gap, 0.5 mile south on USFS 67 and 0.6 mile south on the Trail, is a much better Trailhead. Hikers are advised to use the present U.S. 64 for access to Franklin (see Section Eight).

Deep Gap can be reached by motor vehicles on USFS 71, a one-lane, six-mile-long road leaving U.S. 64 near the Clay-Macon county line.

USFS 67, which starts at Wallace Gap, provides access to the Trail *via* side trails at many points. It changes to gravel just past the Standing Indian Campground and ends at a parking area 0.4 mile from the A.T. west of Albert Mountain.

Maps

USFS map of the Southern Nantahala Wilderness Area, TVA Rainbow Springs and Prentiss quadrangles, and ATC Nantahala National Forest map with this guide.

Shelters, Campsites, and Water

This section has four shelters, all located near water. The spring at Carter Gap Shelter and the stream at Standing Indian Shelter have been reliable, but the springs at Rock Gap Shelter and Big Spring Shelter went dry during a drought in the late 1980s.

At Betty Creek Gap, a seasonal spring is just to the right of the Trail, 50 feet north of the clearing, and a stream is 0.2 mile west on a blue-blazed trail.

The summit area of Standing Indian Mountain is a popular campground, with water available from a fairly reliable spring about 0.2 mile downhill near the junction with Lower Trail Ridge.

Rock Gap and Deep Gap have trash cans.

Public Accommodations and Services

Franklin is 10 miles east of Wallace Gap but is more easily reached from U.S. 64 at Winding Stair Gap, 3.1 miles north on the Trail; see Section Eight.

Standing Indian Campground, a USFS facility, is located 1.5 miles south of Wallace Gap on USFS 67.

Rainbow Springs, a commercial campground, is 1.1 miles west of Wallace Gap on "Old 64" and offers showers, laundry, bunk-house, cabins, food supplies, and shuttle service.

Deep Gap has no public facilities nearby.

Trail Description, North to South

Miles	Data
0.0	The A.T. starts on "Old 64" in Wallace Gap (3,738 feet), just east of paved USFS 67 to **Standing Indian Campground**.
0.6	Reach Rock Gap. To left, blue-blazed trail descends 0.7 mile to the enormous John Wasilik Memorial Poplar, well worth the trip. On right is parking area on USFS 67.
0.7	Reach Trail junction; A.T. bears left and continues uphill. Blue-blazed trail bears right for 300 feet to **Rock Gap Shelter**, with overhang offering additional cooking space sheltered from the rain.
1.1	Seasonal spring 25 feet below Trail. Several seasonal springs are near the Trail for the next 1.5 miles.
3.2	Reach Glassmine Gap in small clearing. On right, blue-blazed Long Branch Trail goes downhill 2.0 miles to USFS 67 near **Standing Indian Campground**.
4.0	Cross stream in wet area.
6.0	Reach Big Spring Gap, where several trails converge. To right, blue-blazed trail leads 280 feet to **Big Spring Shelter**. Water is 75 feet below shelter.
6.4	Reach clearing. Blue-blazed trail on right (old road) is bad-weather detour of Albert Mountain, leading 0.4 mile to parking area at end of USFS 67 and continuing on road another 0.4 mile to rejoin A.T.
6.6	Reach summit of Albert Mountain (5,250 feet). Summit has a firetower and a magnificent view, but no water. Descent of southern slope is very steep and rocky.
6.9	Reach junction with two blue-blazed trails where gravel USFS 67 is a few feet to the right. The Bearpen Trail crosses gravel road and descends to USFS 67, 3.2 miles south of campground area. The Albert Mountain bypass trail follows road uphill to right.

7.3   Trail passes near USFS 67 in Bearpen Gap. During next half-mile, Trail slabs side of Big Butt Mountain with occasional views into Coweeta area.

7.9   Descend log steps, and turn right onto old road, then cross culvert that conducts water from spring above.

8.2   Reach Mooney Gap. Trail crosses USFS 83, which comes up gravel road at left from U.S. 441 and continues right to join USFS 67 in 1.2 miles. Trail enters Southern Nantahala Wilderness Area 200 feet farther.

9.1   Reach Betty Creek Gap. Small spring is located on left just before reaching clearing. Blue-blazed Betty Creek Trail on right leads 0.2 mile to stream and USFS 67, 6.3 miles south of Standing Indian Campground area. A.T. continues across clearing and ascends gradually to Little Ridgepole Mountain.

11.1   Unmarked trail on left leads 25 feet to excellent eastern vista.

11.4   Trail bears right and crosses to Ridgepole Mountain, leaving Nantahalas for the Blue Ridge. Ascend to shoulder of Ridgepole.

12.8   Reach Carter Gap. Follow blue blazes to the new **Carter Gap Shelter** to the left, and spring and old shelter on blue-blazed trail to the right. Spring is 200 feet on blue-blazed trail to right. Trail continues straight through gap.

13.2   Reach junction with Timber Ridge Trail on right. This blue-blazed trail leads 2.3 miles to USFS 67.

14.2   Cross Coleman Gap in dense rhododendron thicket. Cross several small streams on level trail in next mile.

16.0   Reach Beech Gap with side trails and logging roads. Unreliable spring is 100 feet from Trail on left. Blue-blazed trail on right is Beech Gap Trail and leads 2.8 miles to USFS 67. Begin steady climb up Standing Indian Mountain.

18.9   Reach junction with blue-blazed Lower Trail Ridge Trail. To left, this trail leads 600 feet to summit of Standing Indian Mountain. To right, trail leads 4.2 miles to **Standing Indian Campground**. One hundred feet beyond junction, unmarked trail goes right 0.2 mile to spring.

20.4   Blue-blazed side trail on left leads 250 feet to **Standing Indian Shelter**. Water is available from stream reached by side trail to right just beyond shelter trail.

21.3   Leave wilderness area, and enter Deep Gap parking area
        (4,341 feet) on USFS 71, which ends here, six miles from
        U.S. 64. Seasonal water is available 150 feet down blue-
        blazed trail. Blue-blazed Kimsey Creek Trail on right
        follows a gentle grade for 3.7 miles to **Standing Indian
        Campground**. To continue on Trail, go straight across
        parking area.

Trail Description, South to North

Miles   **Data**

0.0   The A.T. leaves Deep Gap (4,341 feet) at end of USFS 71, on
        a graded trail between two logging roads, east of parking
        areas, and enters Southern Nantahala Wilderness Area.
        Seasonal water is available 150 feet down blue-blazed
        trail. Blue-blazed Kimsey Creek Trail to left leads 3.7 miles
        to **Standing Indian Campground**.

0.9   Reach side trail to **Standing Indian Shelter**, 250 feet to
        right of Trail. Water is available from a stream reached by
        short trail to left. A.T. continues climbing steadily on
        grassy road.

2.4   Pass unmarked trail to spring on left. One hundred feet
        farther, reach junction with blue-blazed Lower Trail Ridge
        Trail. To right, this trail leads 600 feet to Standing Indian
        summit. To left, it leads 4.2 miles to **Standing Indian
        Campground**.

5.3   Reach Beech Gap, with side trails. Unreliable seasonal
        water is available 100 feet from Trail to right. To left, blue-
        blazed Beech Gap Trail leads 2.8 miles to USFS 67, four
        miles south of Standing Indian Campground area. In the
        next mile, cross several small streams on nearly level trail.

7.1   Reach Coleman Gap in dense rhododendron thicket.

8.1   Reach blue-blazed Timber Ridge Trail on left. It leads 2.3
        miles to USFS 67, 4.4 miles south of Standing Indian
        Campground area.

8.5   Reach Carter Gap, a large level area with the new **Carter
        Gap Shelter** to the right, and spring and old shelter on

blue-blazed trail to the left. Water is available from a reliable spring on blue-blazed trail 200 feet to left of Trail. From Carter Gap, Trail climbs to shoulder of Ridgepole Mountain.

9.9   Trail bears left onto Little Ridgepole Mountain, leaving the eastern arm of the Blue Ridge to head north along the Nantahala Mountains to the Smokies.

10.2   Unmarked trail on right leads 25 feet to excellent vista.

12.2   Reach Betty Creek Gap. A spring is located just past clearing on right. Blue-blazed trail on left leads 0.2 mile to stream and USFS 67, 6.3 miles south of **Standing Indian Campground** area. A.T. crosses clearing and enters rhododendron tunnel.

13.1   Reach Mooney Gap, and cross USFS 83. To right, a gravel road leads to U.S. 441. To left, it leads to junction with USFS 67. The Trail has now left the Southern Nantahala Wilderness Area.

13.2   Cross culvert that conducts water (spring unreliable) above Trail, then jog left up log steps, leaving old road and climbing on graded trail.

13.4   Trail crosses above cliff while slabbing very steep eastern face of Big Butt Mountain, with some views into Coweeta valley.

14.0   Trail passes near gravel USFS 67 in Bearpen Gap.

14.4   Reach junction with two blue-blazed trails on left. Bearpen Trail goes left across gravel USFS 67 and descends in 2.5 miles to same road in valley below. Albert Mountain bad-weather bypass trail turns right and follows road. The A.T. ahead climbs the steep, rocky, and memorable southern side of Albert Mountain for 0.3 mile.

14.7   Reach summit of Albert Mountain (5,250 feet), with fire-tower and magnificent views (no water).

14.9   At bottom of descent, blue-blazed summit bypass approaches from left. Good spring is 1,000 feet down bypass.

15.3   Reach Big Spring Gap, where several trails converge. To left, blue-blazed trail leads 280 feet to **Big Spring Shelter** and 75 feet farther to water. A.T. bears slightly left and continues on level for next mile.

17.3   Cross stream in wet area.

18.1   Reach Glassmine Gap in small clearing. On left, blue-
        blazed Long Branch Trail descends 2.0 miles to USFS 67.

19.1   Pass seasonal spring left of Trail. Several seasonal sources
        of water are in the next mile.

20.6   Reach blue-blazed trail leading sharply left 300 feet to
        Rock Gap Shelter, with overhang offering additional
        cooking space sheltered from the rain.

20.7   Trail passes parking area at Rock Gap. Paved USFS 67
        leads left 1 mile to **Standing Indian Campground**, with
        restrooms, showers, and pay phone, and right 0.5 mile to
        Wallace Gap. On right, blue-blazed trail leads to the
        enormous John Wasilik Memorial Poplar. A.T. bears
        slightly to right.

21.3   Reach Wallace Gap (3,738 feet). To continue on A.T., climb
        bank on opposite side of "Old 64."

Deep Gap to Bly Gap
Section Ten
6.8 Miles

Brief Description of Section

This section starts at Deep Gap (4,341 feet) and follows the crest of the Blue Ridge, with views to the west of Shooting Creek Valley and Lake Chatuge. In this section, the Trail completes a long curve around the headwaters of the Tallulah River and heads south into Georgia. The Trail climbs steeply over Courthouse Bald from Sassafras Gap on one side and Bly Gap on the other side. This route enters and leaves the Southern Nantahala Wilderness Area twice and remains in wilderness for more than half the section.

Points of Interest

Bly Gap (3,840 feet), with its open view northwest to the Tusquittee Range, is an outstanding feature of the section, as are the views from the crest of the Blue Ridge. A half-mile trail near Muskrat Creek Shelter to Ravenrock Ridge affords an outstanding view.

Road Approaches

Deep Gap is at the end of a six-mile, one-lane gravel road, USFS 71, which leaves U.S. 64 just west of the Clay-Macon county line and five miles west of Winding Stair Gap.

There is no road approach to Bly Gap.

Maps

USFS map of Southern Nantahala Wilderness Area and Standing Indian Basin; TVA Rainbow Springs and Hightower Bald quadrangles; and ATC Nantahala National Forest map with this guide.

Shelters, Campsites, and Water

The only shelter in this section is the Muskrat Creek Shelter, 4.0 miles south of Deep Gap and 2.8 miles north of Bly Gap. Water is located at a spring behind the shelter.

Bly Gap has two springs, one on each side of the Trail, about 100 feet away. Whiteoak Stamp has water and there are a few seasonal springs and streams along this section. A fair spring is located about 400 feet south of Whiteoak Stamp on an unmarked trail.

Public Accommodations and Services

No public accommodations are available in either Deep Gap or Bly Gap.

Precautions

Several trails converge in Bly Gap, and caution must be taken to follow the A.T. To the west is a five-mile route down Eagle Fork of Shooting Creek; it begins as a worn woods road. Another trail, as indicated on the TVA Hightower Bald quadrangle, leads to Tate City on the Tallulah River *via* Fall Branch.

Trail Description, North to South

Miles   **Data**

0.0   The A.T. crosses a parking area at the end of USFS 71 in Deep Gap (4,341 feet), bears right into woods, and begins graded ascent of Yellow Mountain. The blue-blazed Kimsey Creek Trail on right leads 3.7 miles to **Standing Indian Campground**. Seasonal water is available 150 feet down the blue-blazed trail at the edge of an old camping area.

0.7   Trail switches back up rock outcrop.

1.1   Reach view to north and highest point in section.

2.1   Reach Wateroak Gap in small clearing. Trail continues up ridge.

3.0   Junction with blue-blazed Chunky Gal Trail on the right, which leads 5.5 miles to U.S. 64. A.T. bears left.

3.2   Trail crosses edge of large, grassy clearing at Whiteoak Stamp. Unreliable water to the left 400 feet on obscure trail.

4.0   Reach **Muskrat Creek Shelter** (left 100 feet) just before crossing small stream. This shelter has a latrine uphill to the left of the shelter. One hundred feet on A.T. beyond stream, blue-blazed trail leads right about one-half mile to outstanding cliff view on Ravenrock Ridge.

4.1   Just to right of Trail is view to west.

4.3   Cross logs over stream.

4.9   Reach Sassafras Gap. Begin ascent of Courthouse Bald.

5.4   Trail levels. Skirt top of Courthouse Bald, then begin descent.

5.7   Thirty feet to right is fine view into Shooting Creek Valley.

6.0   Trail passes through two small gaps, skirts side of Sharp Top, then resumes steep descent.

6.8   Reach Bly Gap (3,840 feet) in clearing with fine views to north. One spring is to right, 100 feet from edge of clearing, and a second spring is below and to left. To continue on A.T., cross clearing on top of ridge, then make sharp left at far side of clearing.

Trail Description, South to North

Miles   **Data**

0.0   The A.T. enters Bly Gap (3,840 feet) from the south, turns right to cross the clearing, and continues straight up the top of the ridge. Springs are located on the right before clearing, and another spring is 100 feet on left just before starting up ridge.

0.7   Trail levels, then passes through two small gaps before resuming climb.

1.1   Thirty feet to left of Trail is fine lookout into Shooting Creek Valley.

1.2   Trail levels, slabs southern side of Courthouse Bald, then descends.

1.9   Reach Sassafras Gap. Trail begins gentle climb.
2.5   Cross logs over stream.
2.7   Viewpoint just left of Trail.
2.8   Reach junction with blue-blazed trail on left, leading about a half-mile to outstanding views from cliff on Ravenrock Ridge. One hundred feet farther on A.T., cross stream, and reach **Muskrat Creek Shelter,** 100 feet right of Trail in woods. A latrine is 150 feet uphill beyond shelter.
3.6   Trail crosses edge of large, grassy clearing at Whiteoak Stamp. Unreliable water is to right 400 feet on obscure trail.
3.8   A.T. bears right at junction with blue-blazed Chunky Gal Trail, which lead 5.5 miles to U.S. 64.
4.7   Descend into Wateroak Gap. Trail bears slightly left across small clearing. Start gradual ascent of Yellow Mountain.
5.7   Reach view to north (left) and highest point in section.
6.1   Descend rock outcrop *via* switchbacks.
6.8   Reach Deep Gap parking area (4,341 feet) at end of USFS 71, six miles from U.S. 64. Seasonal water is available 150 feet down blue-blazed trail at edge of old camping area. The blue-blazed Kimsey Creek Trail, leading 3.7 miles to **Standing Indian Campground,** begins on the northwestern side of the parking area. The A.T. continues straight across the parking area.

Side Trails in the Nantahalas

Side trails are an outstanding feature of this part of the Appalachian Trail. In conjunction with the A.T., a wide variety of loop hikes of one day or several days can be made. Hikers contemplating loop hikes are urged to acquire the USFS map entitled "Southern Nantahala Wilderness and Standing Indian Basin," which covers the A.T. from Wallace Gap south into Georgia and most of the side trails described below. Most of the trails described are maintained cooperatively by the USFS and the Nantahala Hiking Club.

1. WESSER CREEK TRAIL: This blue-blazed former route of the A.T. is a loop hike using the A.T. to return to starting point.

Miles	Data
0.0	At Nantahala River bridge on U.S. 19, follow U.S. 19 east.
0.9	Turn right into Wesser Creek Road. (Trail not blazed on road.)
2.6	Reach end of road and beginning of graded trail (cars can be driven to this point). Blue blazes commence.
3.0	Reach Wesser Creek and site of former shelter.
4.3	Trail leaves creek and climbs toward Wesser Bald.
6.2	Reach junction with present A.T. on ridge, 0.8 mile north of Wesser Bald, 5.7 miles south of Wesser (see Section Six). Use A.T. (turn right) to return to Wesser. Loop distance is 11.9 miles total.

2. BARTRAM TRAIL: Yellow-blazed Bartram Trail, when complete, will be continuous from South Carolina to Cheoah Bald. Described here is the section between Franklin, North Carolina, and Nantahala Lake. It is worth noting that the section between Wallace Branch and Wayah Bald has more than one mile of ascent.

Miles	Data
0.0	Trailhead on Wallace Branch, on N.C. 1315, 1.7 miles from its junction with "Old 64" on the outskirts of Franklin, near the Wayah District offices of USFS.
1.3	Reach junction with old Trimont Trail from Franklin to Wayah Bald. Bartram Trail turns left.
10.0	Reach junction with A.T., 0.5 mile north of Wayah Bald.
12.4	Bartram Trail turns right and leaves A.T. Descend west on McDonald Ridge.
14.1	Reach paved USFS 711 at Sawmill Gap. Bartram jogs left across road, then continues to N.C. 1310 on the shore of Nantahala Lake.

3. JOHN WASILIK MEMORIAL POPLAR TRAIL: This 0.7-mile blue-blazed trail starts at the Rock Gap trailhead (see Section Nine) and leads downhill to a remarkable tree, the second-largest poplar in the East. The 1.4-mile round trip is well worth the effort to see a tree reminiscent of the sequoia.

4. LONG BRANCH TRAIL: Blue-blazed, 2.0 miles. One of many connecting trails between the Standing Indian Campground area and the A.T. The trailhead is across the road from the Backcountry Information Center on USFS 67 near the campground. It ends on the A.T. at Glassmine Gap, after climbing through hardwood forest on the southern slope of Long Branch Creek. It intersects an orange-blazed horse trail and crosses the creek near the upper end.

5. BEARPEN TRAIL: Blue-blazed, 2.5 miles. This charming connector trail starts on USFS 67, three miles south of the Backcountry Information Center (sign and parking). The lower 0.4 mile follows a grassed logging road. Watch for easy-to-miss turn-off road into woods. The rest of the trail traverses several different kinds of woodland while climbing to meet the A.T. at the southern end of Albert Mountain.

6. BETTY CREEK GAP TRAIL: Blue-blazed, 0.2 mile. This short connector trail leaves USFS 67 at 6.3 miles south of the Backcountry Information Center, crosses a stream, and tunnels through a rhododendron thicket to the A.T. at Betty Creek Gap.

7. TIMBER RIDGE TRAIL: Blue-blazed, 2.3 miles. This trail starts at the Timber Ridge-Big Laurel Falls parking area on USFS 67, 4.4 miles south of the Backcountry Information Center. After crossing a log bridge over a large brook, trail turns left and climbs through rhododendron. About halfway, it crosses Big Laurel Branch on a new log bridge, then climbs to Timber Ridge, where it proceeds through open, fern-covered woods to the A.T., 0.4 mile south of Carter Gap.

8. BEECH GAP TRAIL: Blue-blazed, 2.8 miles. Trail starts at Beech Gap parking area on USFS 67, four miles south of Backcountry Information Center. At 0.5 mile, Big Indian Horse Trail (orange blazes) approaches from right. At 2.0 miles, reach Big Indian Road (where horse trail leaves), and turn left. After pleasant, almost-level road walk, reach A.T. at Beech Gap.

9. LOWER TRAIL RIDGE TRAIL: Blue-blazed, 4.2 miles. This trail is the most direct but a strenuous way to reach Standing Indian Mountain from the Standing Indian Campground. It originates from the Backcountry Information Center, crosses the Nantahala River on the main campground road, skirts the campground area, then climbs rather steeply up Lower Trail Ridge directly to the mountain. It crosses the A.T. near the top of the mountain and continues 0.1 mile to end at the summit clearing.

10. KIMSEY CREEK TRAIL: Blue-blazed, 3.7 miles. This popular trail follows the course of Kimsey Creek from the campground to Deep Gap. It begins at the Backcountry Information Center, crosses the river on the campground road, then turns right, and skirts the campground on the northern side. At 0.3 mile, it turns left and leaves the trails that follow the river. At 0.9 mile, it enters a clearing, where it turns right along a gated road following Kimsey Creek. At 2.1 miles, it crosses a log bridge over a side creek. The trail enters Deep Gap through the old picnic and camping area. Standing Indian Mountain can be reached by turning left on A.T.

11. CHUNKY GAL TRAIL: Blue-blazed, 5.5 miles. This little-used trail (scenic when the trees are without leaves) follows the ridge of Chunky Gal Mountain. Trailhead is on U.S. 64 in Glade Gap, at the top of the long climb out of Shooting Creek Valley. The beginning is marked with a small sign and blazes but is not easy to locate. The trail ends at the A.T. 3.0 miles south of Deep Gap.

The A.T. in the
Chattahoochee National Forest
(Bly Gap, North Carolina, to
Springer Mountain, Georgia)
75.6 Miles

Although northern Georgia is partly within the southern coastal plains geologic region, it offers numerous opportunities for both strenuous and long-distance hiking through primitive mountain wilderness areas. Most of the A.T. in this section is along ridges at elevations around 3,000 feet. Ascents and descents are sometimes steep. Scenic vistas are possible from many rocky overlooks along the Trail and from the summits of several of the mountain peaks. From those vantage points extend the multiple mountain ranges of the southern Appalachians, gentle in contour and soft green in color.

Northern Georgia is Blue Ridge country. The mountains take the form of an enormous V, open to the north. The apex of the V is Springer Mountain, 3,782 feet in height, the southern terminus of the 14-state Appalachian Trail. The Blue Ridge enters Georgia just east of Rich Knob, reaches its southern extremity, and swings back northward.

In the early years of the Appalachian Trail Conference, it was uncertain whether the A.T. in southern North Carolina and Georgia should follow the eastern or the western arm of this V. The eastern arm was finally chosen because of its greater accessibility and the existence of a developed USFS trail system. This selection necessitated crossing over from the range at the southwestern end of the Great Smokies, which is continuous with the western arm of the V. The cross-over route follows the Yellow Creek Mountains, Wauchecha and Cheoah balds, and the Nantahala Mountains.

The southern Appalachian mountain system grows out of the forking of the Blue Ridge in southern Virginia, which, farther north, is a narrow crestline ridge. In southern Virginia, the Blue Ridge forks where the Roanoke River breaks through the range. The eastern range takes a circuitous route far to the east. It is the watershed and contains many outstanding peaks, such as Grand-father, Whiteside, and Caesars Head, but it is inferior to the western range in elevation and general scenic interest. The loftier western range is crossed by several rivers rising in the Blue Ridge and is broken into segments known, respectively, as the Stone, Iron, Unaka, Great Smoky, Unicoi, Frog, Ellijay, and Cohutta mountains. The eastern and western ranges join together at Springer Mountain in Georgia. Cross chains, enclosing beautiful elevated valleys, connect the two master ranges. From the forking of the Blue Ridge in Virginia, the A.T. follows the western range south through the Great Smokies.

Trail Route

Projecting south from Springer Mountain is the Amicalola Range, terminating at Mt. Oglethorpe, the original southern terminus of the A.T. For the first 8.8 miles, this range is used for a blue-blazed approach trail between Amicalola Falls State Park and the A.T. on Springer Mountain.

Mt. Oglethorpe was the terminus when the A.T. was first blazed. During the 1950s, private development and chicken farming in-truded on the wilderness experience of the hiker. In 1958, ATC, at the recommendation of the Georgia Appalachian Trail Club, de-cided to abandon Mt. Oglethorpe to development and to move the southern terminus to Springer Mountain, well within, and pro-tected by, the Chattahoochee National Forest. With this relocation and the continued efforts of the Forest Service, the A.T. in Georgia, including Springer Mountain, now lies wholly within the bound-aries of the forest.

For the most part, the Georgia A.T. was routed over a previously existing Forest Service trail along the Blue Ridge crest. The comple-tion in the spring of 1931 of a 20-mile link north of Tray Mountain allowed the first continuous route from Mt. Oglethorpe, the origi-nal terminus, to the Great Smokies. Only minor relocations since that time have changed the Trail from its original route in Georgia.

In the 1960s, the Georgia A.T. was threatened with extinction by a proposed extension of the Blue Ridge Parkway from its end in North Carolina to a route along the ridgecrest (and along the A.T.) in Georgia to Kennesaw Mountain outside Atlanta. Fortunately, the road was never built. In 1968, Congress designated the A.T. one of the first two national scenic trails and thereby gave it the maximum protection possible under the constraints of the multiple-use concepts and practices other laws demand of the U.S. Forest Service (USFS).

Flora

The Georgia mountains are ablaze in April, May, and June with flowering rhododendrons, mountain laurel, and flame azaleas. A normally high annual rainfall ensures lush vegetation, and fields of ferns and wildflowers. The beauty of the southern forests with flowers and shrubs in full bloom leaves an indelible impression.

Shelters

Including the two on the Approach Trail, the Georgia A.T. has 13 shelters, which are well situated at intervals permitting easy dayhikes. All but one of those shelters are three-sided, open-front types. All are floored and have springs close by. The exception is a two-room stone structure on top of Blood Mountain, which has four sides.

Maintenance

The Georgia A.T. and its shelters are managed by the Georgia Appalachian Trail Club, Inc. (GATC), a club of more than 600 members. Early members of GATC helped survey and construct the first locations of the A.T. in Georgia in the 1920s and 1930s. Thus, the club has a rich heritage and a long tradition of Trail stewardship, one that it has shared over the years with the USFS in the Chattahoochee National Forest. GATC members may be seen most weekends cutting weeds, removing blowdowns, painting blazes, installing water bars, building bridges, and, in general, improving the quality of the Trail and the hiking experience. For a detailed history of the club, see *Friendships of the Trail*, published by the GATC and also available from ATC.

Because volunteers maintain the Trail and shelters, it is important that hikers help by packing out what they pack in, not littering, not abusing or vandalizing structures or signs, not cutting across switchbacks, which are there for a purpose, and "taking only photographs and leaving only footprints." Anyone who desires to be involved in Trail maintenance or the club itself is invited to contact the GATC and to participate in any of its Trail-maintenance or other outings. (Write: Georgia Appalachian Trail Club, Inc., P.O. Box 654, Atlanta, GA 30301.)

Sections Eleven-Seventeen

For convenience, and use in this guidebook, the Georgia A.T. has been divided into the following sections, each accessible by car except for the North Carolina-Georgia line and Springer Mountain:

Section Eleven: Bly Gap, North Carolina, to Dicks Creek Gap (U.S. 76), 8.8 miles.

Section Twelve: Dicks Creek Gap (U.S. 76) to Unicoi Gap (Ga. 75), 16.1 miles.

Section Thirteen: Unicoi Gap (Ga. 75) to Tesnatee Gap (Ga. 348), 14.5 miles.

Section Fourteen: Tesnatee Gap (Ga. 348) to Neels Gap (U.S. 19/129), 5.5 miles.

Section Fifteen: Neels Gap (U.S. 19/129) to Woody Gap (Ga. 60), 10.7 miles.

Section Sixteen: Woody Gap (Ga. 60) to Hightower Gap, 11.9 miles.

Section Seventeen: Hightower Gap to Springer Mountain, 8.1 miles.

Approaches to the southern terminus of the Appalachian Trail and loop hiking in Georgia are covered in separate sections at the end of this part of the guidebook.

Bly Gap, North Carolina, to Dicks Creek Gap (U.S. 76)
Section Eleven
8.8 Miles

Brief Description of Section

This is the northernmost section of the Georgia A.T. Interestingly, Bly Gap is almost exactly the same elevation as Springer Mountain, the southernmost point on the Georgia Trail. Dicks Creek Gap, on the other hand, is the lowest gap crossed by a paved road on the Georgia Trail. Consequently, the elevation gain from south to north on this section is greater than from north to south. The route is a graded trail broken by three gaps: Blue Ridge Gap (3,020 feet), Plumorchard Gap (3,090 feet), and Cowart Gap (2,920 feet).

The division between the Chattahoochee National Forest (Georgia) and the Nantahala National Forest (North Carolina) is at Bly Gap. The TVA Hightower Bald quadrangle indicates that Bly Gap is not on the Georgia-North Carolina line but is a short distance (0.2 mile) north in North Carolina.

From Bly Gap (3,840 feet), the Trail generally follows the crest, descending steadily to Blue Ridge Gap. This section of the A.T. now traverses an area that was congressionally designated as protected wilderness in 1984. This designation determines maintenance and management practices by both the Georgia A.T. Club and the U.S. Forest Service.

From Blue Ridge Gap, the Trail ascends As Knob (3,440 feet) and descends to Plumorchard Gap. It climbs up Buzzard Knob (3,760 feet), down to Cowart Gap, and then to Dicks Creek Gap and U.S. 76 (2,675 feet).

Points of Interest

The highlight of this section is Bly Gap, with its open clearing and views. The mountain range to the northwest is the Tusquitee.

The road in the distance to the right, snaking out of mountains and descending to the valley below, is U.S. 64 through Glade Gap.

Along this section are splendid views to the northeast of the imposing Standing Indian Mountain (5,498 feet), as well as of the Nantahala Mountains in North Carolina. The isolated peak of Hightower Bald (4,568 feet) is conspicuous to the northwest.

Road Approaches

Bly Gap is not accessible by car. It is 6.8 miles north, *via* the A.T., to Deep Gap, North Carolina, and USFS 71 (six miles from U.S. 64) and 3.2 miles south to an almost impassable road in Blue Ridge Gap.

Blue Ridge Gap is crossed by narrow, rutted USFS 72, which is usually passable only by four-wheel-drive vehicles. The road leads 7.5 miles through Titus, Georgia, to U.S. 76, 2.8 miles west of Dicks Creek Gap.

Dicks Creek Gap, the southern end of the section, is on U.S. 76, 18 miles west of Clayton and 11 miles east of Hiawassee, Georgia. Parking is available; fee ($2.00 in 1998).

Maps

USGS Hightower Bald quadrangle; ATC Chattahoochee National Forest map with this guide.

Shelters, Campsites, and Water

The only shelter in this section is Plumorchard Gap Shelter, located near Plumorchard Gap, 4.5 miles south of Bly Gap. Plumorchard Gap Shelter has water, and a second spring is located 0.1 mile from the Trail to the west of Plumorchard Gap. A small stream flows through the picnic area in Dicks Creek Gap.

Public Accommodations and Supplies

No facilities are available in or near Bly Gap.

No public transportation is available in Dicks Creek Gap. The nearest reliable sources of supplies are in Hiawassee, 11 miles west, or in Clayton, 18 miles east. The Blueberry Patch, an organic farm and hostel 3.5 miles west on U.S. 76, offers lodging, shower, laundry, and shuttle services, and some services to northbound thru-hikers February 15 to May 15 and to southbound thru-hikers on request; (706) 896-4893.

Precautions

Several trails converge in Bly Gap, and caution must be taken to follow the A.T. To the west is a five-mile route down Eagle Fork of Shooting Creek; it begins as a worn woods road. Another trail leads to the valley along the Tallulah River.

Trail Description, North to South

Miles	Data
0.0	From open ridge in Bly Gap (3,840 feet), descend slightly, and turn sharply left. Descend about 100 yards, then turn right on graded trail. A spring is located several yards to left and downhill at this turn.
0.2	Cross North Carolina-Georgia state line (unmarked) while swinging around eastern side of Rich Knob (4,132 feet).
0.7	Reach ridgetop. Follow along narrow crest. Cross over small knob through laurel and rhododendron. Just over top is rock outcrop on right with views of the valley and Hightower Bald to far right. Cross over ridge, and continue descent.
1.3	Reach level section. Obscure trail on right leads one mile to headwaters of Hightower Creek. Cross over small knob through laurel and rhododendron.
1.8	Bear to left side of ridge, skirting eastern side of Rocky Knob (3,560 feet).
2.0	Reach Rich Cove Gap (3,400 feet). Cross to right side of ridge, and continue descent.
2.6	Regain ridgecrest, then descend steadily.
3.2	Reach Blue Ridge Gap (3,020 feet) and dirt road, usually impassable by two-wheel-drive automobiles. Cross road, and ascend.

3.8 Reach high point of As Knob (3,440 feet). Beyond, cross small knob, and cross to eastern side of ridge.

4.0 Begin steady descent.

4.5 Reach Plumorchard Gap (3,090 feet). To left (east), side trail leads approximately 0.2 mile to **Plumorchard Gap Shelter**, built in 1993 by GATC and USFS. Water may be found at the creek that crosses trail to shelter. A spring is about 600 feet from A.T. on trail to right, west, from gap. Below shelter, side trail leads down Plumorchard Creek about three miles to road at Plumorchard Church. In Plumorchard Gap, old trail to right, west, leads down Big John Creek to Pleasant Hill School at road on Hightower Creek. From Plumorchard Gap, A.T. ascends along western slope. Green moss, laurel, and rhododendron cover rocky slopes above the Trail.

5.3 Reach crest of ridge. Beyond, skirt left side of ridge, then right side, descending.

5.6 Reach Bull Gap (3,550 feet). Ascend around eastern side of Buzzard Knob (3,760 feet).

5.9 Begin steady descent along, or just below, narrow ridgecrest.

7.0 Reach Cowart Gap (2,920 feet), with stand of tall pines. Old, impassable road between Hightower Creek and Holden Branch crosses Trail. Ascend on right side of ridge.

7.5 Cross to left side of ridge, and skirt southern side of Little Bald Knob (3,440 feet).

7.7 Cross over spur (3,160 feet). Water is located north on Trail and downhill about 600 feet.

8.4 Reach small gap. Ascend, and cross over shoulder of ridge.

8.8 Descend through picnic area, and reach Dicks Creek Gap (2,675 feet) and U. S. 76; parking available. To continue on A.T., cross highway.

Trail Description, South to North

Miles   **Data**

0.0   From highway in Dicks Creek Gap (2,675 feet), follow
       Trail through picnic area, and ascend along stream up
       ravine. Reach ridgecrest. Cross over shoulder of ridge.
0.4   At small gap, bear right from crest, skirting southern side
       of Little Bald Knob (3,440 feet).
1.1   Cross over spur (3,160 feet). Water is available ahead on
       Trail and downhill about 600 feet.
1.3   Reach ridgecrest. Beyond, descend.
1.8   Reach Cowart Gap (2,920 feet), with stand of tall pines.
       Located here is an abandoned crossroad. From Cowart
       Gap, ascend steadily on left side of ridge.
2.2   Cross to right side of ridge with knob on left. Continue
       below ridge, then ascend generally along narrow crest,
       with fine views on both sides in winter.
3.0   Pass to right of Buzzard Knob (3,760 feet). Descend.
3.2   Reach Bull Gap (3,550 feet). Ascend, bearing to left and
       then right side of ridgetop. Descend to left of ridge. Green
       moss, laurel, and rhododendron cover rocky slopes above
       Trail.
4.3   Reach Plumorchard Gap (3,090 feet). This is the midpoint
       of the section. To right (east), blue-blazed trail leads about
       0.2 mile to **Plumorchard Gap Shelter**, with stream. A
       spring is approximately 600 feet from A.T. on trail to left
       of gap. Below shelter, trail leads down Plumorchard Creek
       about three miles to road at Plumorchard Church. In
       Plumorchard Gap, old trail to left, west, leads down Big
       John Creek to Pleasant Hill School at road on Hightower
       Creek. From Plumorchard Gap, A.T. ascends toward sum-
       mit of As Knob.
4.8   Reach crest of As Knob. Descend, and ascend slightly.
5.0   Reach high point of As Knob (3,440 feet). Descend.
5.6   Reach Blue Ridge Gap (3,020 feet) and dirt road, usually
       impassable by two-wheel-drive automobiles. Cross road,
       and ascend, following wide trail.
6.2   Bear to left of ridge, swinging around western side of
       Wheeler Knob (3,560 feet).

6.8 Reach ridgecrest at Rich Cove Gap (3,400 feet). Ascend to right of ridge, skirting eastern side of Rocky Knob (3,560 feet). Regain ridgetop. Cross over small knob.

7.5 In wide, level section, obscure trail on left leads one mile to headwaters of Hightower Creek. Along this section in the fall and winter are views of Hightower Bald on left. Ascend, continuing along narrow ridgetop. Descend, then cross over small knob. Near top is rock outcrop on left with fine views.

8.1 Bear to right of ridgecrest, skirting eastern side of Rich Knob.

8.6 Cross Georgia-North Carolina state line (unmarked). Turn left uphill, then right at top of ridge. Spring is located several yards to the right and downhill at left turn on A.T.

8.8 Reach cleared crest of Bly Gap (3,840 feet). The A.T. continues along crest straight ahead and climbs towards Sharp Top. An old road crosses the gap from west to east, leading east to the Tallulah River Valley. Springs are located on the right before clearing, and another spring is 100 feet on left just before starting up ridge.

Dicks Creek Gap (U.S. 76)
to Unicoi Gap (Ga. 75)
Section Twelve
16.1 Miles

Brief Description of Section

While much of this section is on well-graded trail, it contains some of the longest climbs and highest peaks of any Georgia section.

From Dicks Creek Gap (2,675 feet), the Trail ascends Powell Mountain (3,850 feet) and Kelly Knob (4,276 feet), then loses elevation through a series of ascents and descents until it reaches "The Swag of the Blue Ridge" (3,400 feet), a wide, low section. Beyond, the Trail ascends Tray Mountain (4,430 feet), descends to Indian Grave Gap (3,113 feet), and climbs Rocky Mountain (4,017 feet), before descending to Unicoi Gap (2,949 feet).

The Trail between Addis Gap and Tray Gap is now included in the Bobcat Wilderness Area.

Points of Interest

The major points of interest are Tray Mountain (4,430 feet), with a splendid viewpoint, and "The Swag of the Blue Ridge" (3,400 feet), a long, broad ridgecrest with only moderate elevation change for more than three miles.

In the 1960s, when the Georgia A.T. was threatened with extinction by a proposed extension of the Blue Ridge Parkway, GATC battled doggedly for, and won, preservation of "The Swag of the Blue Ridge" because of its unique qualities. Since the 1968 passage of the National Trails System Act and the designation of the Appalachian Trail as the first national scenic trail, the Georgia A.T., including the Swag, has been afforded protection from roads and other development.

The crest of Tray Mountain (4,430 feet) offers superb vistas to the south and southeast. Tray Mountain is probably the southernmost breeding area in the United States for Canada warblers. Directly south is Yonah Mountain. The isolated peak to the southeast is Curruhee Mountain, near Toccoa, Georgia. Farther north on the Trail are views of the Blue Ridge. Brasstown Bald, the highest peak in Georgia, is the prominent peak to the northwest. Rabun Bald, the second-highest peak, is to the northeast. The Nantahala Range can be seen directly to the north in North Carolina.

Between Tray Gap and Indian Grave Gap is an area called the "cheese factory." This was the site of a remote mountain farm operated by a transplanted New Englander in the early nineteenth century. For an interesting account of the old "cheese factory" and of "Trail Mountain" (Tray Mountain), read Charles Lanman's *Letters from the Allegheny Mountains*, published in 1849.

Road Approaches

Dicks Creek Gap is located on U.S. 76, 18 miles west of Clayton and 11 miles east of Hiawassee, which have most services.

In Addis Gap, 5.3 miles south of Dicks Creek Gap, a fire road, USFS 26, leads east about eight miles to Ga. 197 at Wildcat Creek near Lake Burton. To the west of Addis Gap, the road, impassable by car near the gap, leads about five miles to Ga. 75 north of Unicoi Gap.

Unpaved USFS 79 leads southeast from Tray Gap to join the Clarkesville-Lake Burton Road (Ga. 197). To the southwest, it leads to Ga. 75, north of Robertstown. This road was an old circuit road connecting Helen with Clarkesville and is usually passable by cars.

In Indian Grave Gap, unpaved, rough USFS 283 leads left (when hiking north to south) to the Tray Mountain Road (USFS 79) from Ga. 75, north of Robertstown to Tray Gap, and right to Ga. 75 north of Unicoi Gap.

The southern end of this section, Unicoi Gap, is located on Ga. 75, 10 miles north of Helen and 14 miles south of Hiawassee. Parking is available.

Maps

USGS Tray Mountain and Macedonia (old Osborne) quadrangles and the ATC Chattahoochee National Forest map.

Shelters, Campsites, and Water

This section has two shelters. Deep Gap Shelter is 3.5 miles south of Dicks Creek Gap and approximately 0.3 mile from the A.T. at the gap. Tray Mountain Shelter, near the summit of Tray Mountain, is 10.6 miles from the northern end of the section.

Good water sources are adjacent to both shelters. In addition, several streams cross the Trail. Water also can be found at Addis Gap.

At the site of the old "cheese factory" near Tray Mountain Road is a spring.

Public Accommodations and Supplies

At the northern end, in Dicks Creek Gap, it is 11 miles west to Hiawassee and 18 miles east to Clayton for supplies. The Blueberry Patch, an organic farm 3.5 miles west on U.S. 76, offers lodging (hostel), laundry, shower, breakfast, and shuttle back to the A.T. only February 15 to May 15 and to southbound thru-hikers on request; (706) 896-4893.

At the southern end, Unicoi Gap, it is eight miles south to Robertstown, nine miles south to Helen, with all services, and 14 miles north to Hiawassee for supplies.

No public transportation is available through either Dicks Creek Gap or Unicoi Gap. Call ATC headquarters, (304) 535-6331, for a list of available shuttles.

Trail Description, North to South

Miles   **Data**

0.0   From U.S. 76 in Dicks Creek Gap (2,675 feet), follow Trail
        south on old road for about 50 yards. Bear left off road, and
        ascend gradually on right side of ridge, then on left side.
        In first mile, cross several small streams. Pass to left (east)
        of Snake Mountain.

1.2   Reach Moreland Gap (3,050 feet). Obscure trail to right
        (west) leads from Moreland Gap along Swallow Creek

about five miles to Lower Hightower Church at the Osborne settlement on U.S. 76. From Moreland Gap, bear left, ascending steadily on left (eastern) side of ridge. Continue on more gradual slope along broad ridgetop.

2.2   Reach top of Powell Mountain (3,850 feet). Descend slightly.

2.4   Reach McClure Gap. Ascend. At top of slope, blue-blazed trail to left leads to fine view. Continue along ridgetop. Pass to left of Wolfstake Knob, then to right of Whiteoak Stamp. Descend.

3.5   Reach Deep Gap (3,550 feet). Look for blue-blazed trail to left leading 0.3 mile to **Deep Gap Shelter** and spring. On Trail, ascend steadily, and pass to right of Dismal Knob.

4.0   Cross to left side of ridge in shallow gap.

4.2   Reach crest of Kelly Knob. Summit (4,276 feet) is about 0.2 mile to right. This is the highest peak between the North Carolina line and Tray Mountain and one of the two peaks of Double Spring Knob. Descend steadily around southwest slope. Cross over small knoll.

5.3   Reach Addis Gap (3,304 feet). Water may still be found 0.5 mile from fire road to the left at old shelter site. From gap, begin ascent along ridgecrest, soon swinging to right (western) side of ridge.

5.9   Return to ridgecrest, and begin descent.

6.1   Cross Sassafras Gap (3,500 feet). Spring is about 150 yards downhill to left (east). Ascend around left side of ridge. Regain ridgetop, and continue to ascend around eastern side of Round Top (3,964 feet).

6.5   Cross over shoulder of Round Top, and descend. Continue along ridgetop, generally descending.

7.2   Cross Blue Ridge Swag (3,400 feet), lowest gap in this section. Begin long climb, generally ascending on or just below ridgecrest.

8.4   Swing around right (western) side of Young Lick Knob (3,800 feet). Descend along eastern side of ridge.

8.9   Reach Steeltrap Gap (3,500 feet). Ascend, then descend.

9.4   Pass Wolfpen Gap (3,550 feet). Ascend, pass to right of knob, and descend.

10.1   Reach gap (3,760 feet). Begin ascent of Tray Mountain, along left (eastern) side of ridge.

10.6   Reach junction of A.T. with blue-blazed trail to right, which leads about 0.2 mile to **Tray Mountain Shelter**, built by USFS in 1971. On right of blue-blazed trail are excellent views from the rocky ledges. Spring is approximately 800 feet downhill to right of shelter. Bear left on Trail, and continue ascent.

10.9   Reach small, rocky summit of Tray Mountain (4,430 feet), with excellent views. This is an outstanding peak of the Georgia Blue Ridge. Descend by switchbacks.

11.7   Reach Tray Mountain Road, USFS 79, in Tray Gap (3,847 feet). Cross road, and enter woods on path to left of parking area. Continue along ridge.

11.9   Rocky cliff overlook to the left, with fall and winter views. Descend.

12.5   Reach gap. To right is site of the old "cheese factory." (See "Points of Interest.") Farther right about 50 yards is Tray Mountain Road with a spring. Ascend slightly, then descend through laurel and rhododendron thickets.

12.7   Cross Tray Mountain Road, USFS 79. Continue descent.

13.4   Reach unpaved road in Indian Grave Gap (3,113 feet). To right along road is blue-blazed trail, which rejoins A.T. in about 1.8 miles, just north of Unicoi Gap. (This blue-blazed trail and the A.T. provide an excellent one-day loop hike.) Cross road, and ascend around southern side of ridge.

14.0   Come into small saddle, bear left, and begin ascent of Rocky Mountain. Cross to southern side of ridge, where rocky slopes afford views to south.

14.8   Reach summit of Rocky Mountain (4,017 feet). Continue along crest; descend.

15.2   Pass junction with side (blue-blazed) trail, which leads back to Indian Grave Gap.

15.5   Cross stream.

16.1   Reach Unicoi Gap (2,949 feet) and Ga. 75. To continue on A.T., go to northern end of parking area, and cross highway.

Trail Description, South to North

Miles   **Data**

0.0   From Ga. 75 in Unicoi Gap (2,949 feet), cross to southern
       end of parking area, climb several steps, and ascend,
       climbing steadily along left side of ridge.

0.6   Reach stream that crosses Trail. Continue climb.

0.9   Reach shoulder (3,600 feet) of Rocky Mountain. Blue-
       blazed trail to left leads westward and reconnects with
       A.T. in Indian Grave Gap. This blue-blazed trail, together
       with the A.T., makes an excellent one-day loop hike. To
       continue on Trail, bear right, and climb steadily.

1.2   Reach crestline of Rocky Mountain (3,960 feet). Continue
       on crest.

1.3   Reach summit of Rocky Mountain (4,017 feet). Bear slightly
       to right, leaving crest, and descend along southern side of
       ridge. Rocky slopes afford views to south. Cross to north-
       ern side of ridge, and descend more steeply.

2.1   Reach small saddle, bear right, and continue descent
       around southern side of ridge.

2.7   Reach unpaved road in Indian Grave Gap (3,113 feet). To
       left along road is a blue-blazed trail that rejoins A.T. just
       north of Unicoi Gap. Cross road, and ascend gradually
       through rhododendron, laurel thickets, and beds of galax.

3.4   Cross Tray Mountain Road, USFS 79. Continue to climb,
       then descend slightly.

3.6   Reach open gap. To left of Trail is the site of the old "cheese
       factory"—see "Points of Interest." To left about 200 feet is
       Tray Mountain Road. Nearby is a spring. Ascend, and
       continue on ridge.

4.2   Reach rocky cliff and overlook to the right of Trail, with
       fall and winter views.

4.4   Reach road, USFS 79, in Tray Gap (3,847 feet). Cross road,
       and ascend by switchbacks.

5.2   Reach open, rocky summit of Tray Mountain (4,430 feet),
       with excellent views. Beyond, Trail is rough, rocky, and
       steep.

5.5   Reach blue-blazed trail that leads approximately 0.2 mile
       to **Tray Mountain Shelter**, built by USFS. Spring is ap-
       proximately 800 feet downhill to right of shelter. Bear
       right on Trail, and descend.

6.0   Reach gap (3,760 feet). Pass to left of knob, and descend.

6.7   Pass Wolfpen Gap (3,550 feet). Skirt western side of ridge,
       and descend.

7.2   Pass Steeltrap Gap (3,500 feet). Ascend along eastern side
       of ridge.

7.7   Swing around left (western) side of Young Lick Knob
       (3,800 feet). Continue along ridge.

8.5   Begin descent into the "Swag of the Blue Ridge."

8.9   Cross Blue Ridge Swag (3,400 feet), lowest gap in the
       general area. Continue along ridge, generally ascending.

9.6   Continue around right (eastern) side of Round Top (3,964
       feet), which is the eastern peak of Dismal Mountain.
       Regain ridgetop, and descend on eastern side of ridge.

10.0   Reach Sassafras Gap (3,500 feet). Off Trail to right, or
       northeast, is spring about 150 yards downhill. After round-
       ing ridge, descend.

10.8   Reach Addis Gap (3,304 feet). A shelter was formerly
       located 0.5 mile down fire road to right; water may still be
       found there. To continue on A.T. from Addis Gap, cross
       over knoll, then begin long climb up ridge to Kelly Knob.

11.9   Reach crest of Kelly Knob (4,276 feet), highest peak be-
       tween Tray Mountain and North Carolina line and one of
       the two peaks of Double Spring Knob. Summit is about 0.2
       mile to left. Descend right (eastern) side of ridge.

12.1   In shallow gap, cross to left (western) side of ridge. Pass to
       left of Dismal Knob.

12.6   Descend to Deep Gap (3,550 feet). Look for blue-blazed
       trail to right leading about 0.3 mile to **Deep Gap Shelter**
       and spring. Continue straight ahead from Deep Gap,
       passing first to left of Whiteoak Stamp, then to right of
       Wolf Stake Knob. Follow ridgecrest.

13.5   Reach blue-blazed trail to right leading to fine view.
       Descend.

13.7   Reach McClure Gap.

13.9   Reach broad top of Powell Mountain (3,850 feet). From top, descend around right (eastern) side.

14.9   After long descent, enter Moreland Gap (3,050 feet). Obscure trail to left leads along Swallow Creek for about five miles to Lower Hightower Church at the Osborne settlement on U.S. 76. From Moreland Gap, bear right, descend along old roadbed, and continue on eastern side of Snake Mountain. Cross several small streams in last mile of descent.

16.1   Reach Dicks Creek Gap (2,675 feet) and U.S. 76. State highway department picnic area is located in gap. To continue on A.T., cross highway, and ascend along stream.

Unicoi Gap (Ga. 75) to
Tesnatee Gap (Ga. 348)
Section Thirteen
14.5 Miles

Brief Description of Section

Viewed north to south, the Blue Ridge turns northwest, then southwest to form the upper rim of a huge bowl, enclosing the headwaters of the Chattahoochee River, the water source for Atlanta, the capital of Georgia, as well as many other municipalities.

This section traverses broad and narrow ridgetops and uses well-defined trails and sections of abandoned fire roads. There are several long climbs, with elevations varying from 2,949 feet at Unicoi Gap to 4,025 feet at Blue Mountain.

From Unicoi Gap, the Trail makes a steep ascent over Blue Mountain in about 1.4 miles, then descends past Rocky Knob to Chattahoochee Gap (3,500 feet). Beyond, the Trail swings southwest, skirts Horsetrough Mountain, and drops into Poplar Stamp Gap (3,350 feet). It then follows an abandoned road to Low Gap (3,050 feet) and continues up and down, with elevations ranging from 3,650 feet on Poor Mountain to 3,150 feet in Wide Gap. There, the Trail turns west and descends to Wolfpen Stamp (3,600 feet) and Hogpen Gap (3,450 feet). It then climbs gradually over Wildcat Mountain and descends to Tesnatee Gap (3,138 feet) and Ga. 348.

The Trail between Unicoi Gap and Hogpen Gap, and some of the Trail between Hogpen Gap and Tesnatee Gap, is now included in a congressionally designated wilderness area, a decision that determines maintenance and management practices by both the Georgia A.T. Club and the U.S. Forest Service.

Points of Interest

One site of interest is Chattahoochee Spring, headwaters of the Chattahoochee River and the drinking-water source for millions of residents. From Chattahoochee Gap, location of the spring, a 5.3-mile blue-blazed side trail leads around Jacks Knob to Brasstown Bald, Georgia's highest mountain.

An abandoned road that enters Tesnatee Gap from the south is reputed to be one of the oldest in the region. It is impassable by car but was once a toll road over the mountain before the Neels Gap (Frogtown Gap) highway was built near the end of the nineteenth century. Charles Lanman, in his *Letters from the Allegheny Mountains*, wrote of stopping overnight in April 1848 at the cabin of a poor farmer in Tesnatee Gap. Lanman was on an exploratory journey to "Track Rock" from Logan's Plantation near Dahlonega, Georgia.

Until 1966, the Trail from Unicoi Gap to Neels Gap was the longest section of the A.T. in Georgia not crossed by a paved highway. That year, the Richard B. Russell Scenic Highway, Ga. 348, was built from Ga. 356, northwest of Robertstown, about 15 miles to Ga. 180.

Unicoi Gap was first crossed by an old Indian trail. Later, it was the route for the first road built across the mountain range. It is now crossed by a major highway, Ga. 75. A spring, the headwaters of the Hiawassee River, is located east of Ga. 75 and north of Unicoi Gap about 400 yards.

Road Approaches

Unicoi Gap, the northern end of the section, is located on Ga. 75, about nine miles north of Helen. To the north of Unicoi Gap, it is 14 miles to Hiawassee.

Poplar Stamp Gap, eight miles from Unicoi Gap, may be approached but not reached from Ga. 358, off Ga. 75, north of Robertstown.

Hogpen Gap, 13.6 miles south of Unicoi Gap, is crossed by Ga. 348 (the Richard B. Russell Scenic Highway), which extends approximately 15 miles from Ga. 356 (northwest of Robertstown) to Ga. 180. Parking is available here and at Tesnatee Gap.

Tesnatee Gap, the southern end of this section, is also crossed by Ga. 348, north of Hogpen Gap. (To reach Hogpen Gap and Tesnatee Gap, go north on Ga. 75 in Robertstown, turn left across the Chattahoochee River bridge onto Ga. 356, and, in 2.5 miles, turn

right onto Ga. 348.) It is about 10 miles from Robertstown to
Hogpen Gap and 0.7 mile by road farther to Tesnatee Gap.

Maps

USGS Cowrock, Jacks Gap, and Tray Mountain quadrangles,
and the ATC Chattahoochee National Forest map.

Shelters, Campsites, and Water

This section has three shelters. Blue Mountain Shelter is 2.2 miles
from Unicoi Gap, and Low Gap Shelter is 9.4 miles. The Whitley
Gap Shelter is located 1.2 miles down a blue-blazed side trail, which
intersects the A.T. about 0.2 mile south of Hogpen Gap (Ga. 348), or
13.8 miles south of Unicoi Gap.

Water is located 0.2 mile north on the Trail, is 3.1 miles south of
Unicoi Gap.

Springs are located near the Blue Mountain Shelter, at Rocky
Knob, at Chattahoochee Gap, at Low Gap near the Low Gap Shelter,
and near the Whitley Gap Shelter.

Public Accommodations and Supplies

No bus lines operate through either Unicoi Gap or Tesnatee Gap.

From Unicoi Gap, the nearest stores and supplies are in
Robertstown, about eight miles south on Ga. 75. Helen, another
mile south on Ga. 75, has motels, groceries, shops, laundromat, post
office, and shuttle services.

Trail Description, North to South

Miles   Data

0.0   At northern end of parking area in Unicoi Gap (2,949 feet),
       cross highway, and ascend on long switchback paralleling
       highway. Climb log steps, turn right, and continue ascent
       along rocky trail.
1.2   Reach ridgecrest.

1.4   Reach top of Blue Mountain (4,025 feet). Descend, and continue along narrow crest, alternately ascending and descending.

2.2   Reach blue-blazed trail to **Blue Mountain Shelter** (built in 1988 by GATC and USFS). Spring on the the right 0.1 mile south on A.T.

2.6   Pass Henson Gap (3,550 feet), named for man who was ambushed and killed here many years ago.

2.7   Reach large, flat area. Stream is approximately 150 yards down slope; spring is 0.2 mile ahead on Trail.

2.9   Spring is several yards to right of Trail, down rocky slope. Continue around Rocky Knob (4,015 feet). Cross several rock slides, and continue on northern side of ridge.

3.8   Enter Red Clay Gap (3,450 feet). Continue on left side of ridge.

4.2   Bear right, and ascend gradually.

4.4   Reach Chattahoochee Gap (3,500 feet). Chattahoochee Spring, source of Chattahoochee River, is about 200 yards down steep blue-blazed trail to the left. Blue-blazed trail entering gap from right leads around Jacks Knob and out Hiawassee Ridge about 2.4 miles to Jacks Gap on Ga. 180 and then to the top of Brasstown Bald. Avoid old road on left, and continue ascending along side of ridge. Descend following narrow ridgetop.

5.1   Reach flat area on ridgetop.

5.2   Begin sharp climb to top of knoll, then descend.

5.6   Reach Cold Springs Gap (3,450 feet). (No spring here.) Bear to left of ridge, and follow old road for next 3.8 miles to Low Gap. Skirt southeastern side of Horsetrough Mountain (4,045 feet). Several small streams cross road.

7.5   Cross shoulder, and descend.

8.0   Reach Poplar Stamp Gap (3,350 feet). Stream is several hundred feet down old road to left. Continue south along fire road.

9.4   Reach Low Gap (3,050 feet). **Shelter** and stream are about 200 feet to left (east). Two old trails, which may be indistinct and impassable, lead into the valley to right (west). Those trails converge at Stink Creek and connect with an old road that leads out to Choestoe. Follow Trail south up slope. Climb steadily.

10.0   Reach flat, rocky summit of Sheep Rock Top (3,575 feet). Descend, and continue along narrow ridge, alternately ascending and descending.

11.1   Enter Wide Gap (3,150 feet). (A trail, no longer visible from the A.T., enters from the right, and leads out to old Tesnatee Gap-Choestoe Road.) Begin long ascent along narrow ridge.

11.7   Reach top of Poor Mountain (3,650 feet). Descend along western side of ridge.

12.0   Enter Sapling Gap (3,450 feet). Continue on Trail, crossing to left side of ridge.

12.4   Pass to left of Strawberry Top (3,710 feet).

12.7   Reach ridgecrest at White Oak Stamp. Continue along crest, passing to left of Wolfpen Stamp (3,600 feet).

13.6   Reach Hogpen Gap and Richard B. Russell Scenic Highway (Ga. 348). (North on highway about 0.1 mile is a superb view of the mountains, including Brasstown Bald, as well as Lordamercy Cove just below road.) In parking area, turn left, and parallel highway for about 200 feet. Cross highway, and begin ascent of Wildcat Mountain. On left is blue-blazed side trail that leads to water.

13.8   On top of ridge, reach sign and blue-blazed trail to the left leading 1.2 miles to **Whitley Gap Shelter** (built by USFS in 1974). To reach shelter, follow blue-blazed trail along ridgetop through laurel and rhododendron, then descend steeply to shelter. About 0.3 mile behind shelter is a spring. To continue on Trail, follow ridge north for 0.1 mile, and begin descent.

14.0   Reach rock cliff with view of Cowrock Mountain to west and 1,200-feet deep gorge of Town Creek between. Descent is steep.

14.5   Reach Tesnatee Gap (3,138 feet) and Ga. 348 again. To continue on Trail, cross parking area, and begin climb.

Trail Description, South to North

Miles   **Data**

0.0   From Ga. 348 in Tesnatee Gap (3, 138 feet), ascend Wildcat
      Mountain by switchbacks, passing large boulders and
      rock outcropping.

0.5   Reach rock cliff with view of Cowrock Mountain to west
      and Town Creek Valley below. Continue along ridge.

0.7   Reach sign and blue-blazed trail to right leading 1.2 miles
      to **Whitley Gap Shelter.** (To reach shelter, follow blue-
      blazed trail along ridgetop through laurel and rhododen-
      dron. Magnificent views in season from ridgetop. De-
      scend steeply to shelter. About 0.3 mile behind shelter is a
      spring.)

0.9   Reach Hogpen Gap (3,450 feet) and Richard B. Russell
      Scenic Highway (Ga. 348). Cross highway, turn left, par-
      allel highway, and continue to northern end of parking
      area. (North on highway about 0.1 mile is a superb view of
      mountains, including Brasstown Bald, and Lordamercy
      Cove just below road. In winter, springs above road form
      icy cliffs.) To continue on Trail, ascend short ramp, and
      follow ridgecrest, passing to right of Wolfpen Stamp
      (3,600 feet).

1.8   Reach White Oak Stamp. Bear to right, and continue on
      eastern side of ridge.

2.1   Pass to right of Strawberry Top (3,710 feet).

2.5   Enter Sapling Gap (3,450 feet). Beyond, ascend along
      western side of ridge.

2.8   Reach summit of Poor Mountain (3,650 feet). Descend,
      and continue along narrow ridgecrest.

3.4   Pass Wide Gap (3,150 feet). An old trail, no longer visible
      from A.T., enters from left. This trail leads to old Tesnatee-
      Choestoe road. Ascend, then alternately descend and
      ascend along narrow crest.

4.5   Pass summit of Sheep Rock Top (3,575 feet). Begin long
      descent.

5.1 Reach Low Gap (3,050 feet). Spring and **shelter** about 200 feet to right (east). Bear to right, and follow wide trail around eastern side of ridge for next 1.4 miles.

5.5 Stream crosses under road.

6.5 Enter Poplar Stamp Gap (3,350 feet). Stream is several hundred feet down old road to the right. Continue on old road, and climb gradually for approximately 0.5 mile, skirting eastern side of Horsetrough Mountain at about 3,500-foot elevation.

7.0 Reach shoulder, and descend gradually. Several small streams cross road.

8.9 Reach Cold Springs Gap (3,450 feet). (No spring here.) Proceed straight ahead, leaving remains of old road on right. Ascend.

9.1 Reach top of knoll, and descend along ridge.

9.3 Reach flat area.

9.4 Bear left, and ascend, following narrow ridgecrest.

10.1 Reach Chattahoochee Gap (3,500 feet). Chattahoochee Spring, source of Chattahoochee River, is about 200 yards down slope on a blue-blazed trail. In the gap, blue-blazed trail straight ahead up ridge leads around Jacks Knob and out Hiawassee Ridge about 2.4 miles to Jacks Gap on Ga. 180, then to the top of Brasstown Bald. From Chattahoochee Gap, continue to right along southern side of ridge.

10.7 Reach Red Clay Gap (3,450 feet). Bear right, and continue through laurel thicket, crossing several rock slides. Swing around to the left side of Rocky Knob (4,015 feet).

11.6 Spring is several yards to the left of Trail down rocky slope.

11.8 Reach large, flat area. Stream is approximately 150 yards down slope on left.

11.9 Pass Henson Gap (3,550 feet), named for a man who was ambushed and killed here many years ago. Beyond, ascend on northern side of ridge.

12.2 Spring on left of Trail.

12.3 Reach side trail to **Blue Mountain Shelter** (built in 1988 by GATC and USFS). Continue on Trail along ridge, which becomes narrow with steep sides. Alternately descend and ascend.

13.1   Reach crest of Blue Mountain (4,025 feet). Descend gradually.
13.3   Bear left of ridge. Continue descent.
14.3   Turn left down slope. Follow long switchback that parallels highway.
14.5   Reach Unicoi Gap (2,949 feet) and Ga. 75; parking available.

Tesnatee Gap (Ga. 348) to Neels Gap (U.S. 19/129)
Section Fourteen
5.5 Miles

Brief Description of Section

The A.T. in this section generally follows broad, rocky tops along a well-defined route. West from Tesnatee Gap (3,138 feet), the Trail ascends Cowrock Mountain (3,842 feet), descends to Swaim Gap (3,450 feet), then climbs over Levelland Mountain (3,942 feet), and finally drops to Neels Gap (3,125 feet) and U.S. 19/129.

This whole section is included in a congressionally designated wilderness area.

Points of Interest

This section has several excellent viewpoints, including rock outcroppings on Cowrock Mountain and Wolf Laurel Top, as well as Levelland Mountain (in fall and winter). The view from Cowrock is especially good. From the height of the mountain, one looks down into the gorge of Town Creek, bound by the north-south ridges of Cowrock Mountain and Wildcat Mountain to the east. The view to the southeast from Cowrock Mountain includes Yonah Mountain, with its unusual, steep rock face. To the north is Brasstown Bald, with its tower and buildings.

Road Approaches

The northern end of the section, Tesnatee Gap, is located on Ga. 348 (the Richard B. Russell Scenic Highway). To reach Tesnatee Gap, go north on Ga. 75 in Robertstown, turn left across the Chattahoochee River bridge onto Ga. 356 and, in 2.5 miles, turn right onto Ga. 348. It is 10 miles from Robertstown to Hogpen Gap and 0.7 mile by road farther to Tesnatee Gap.

The southern end of the section, Neels Gap, is located on U.S. 19/ 129, 19 miles north of Cleveland and 22 miles north of Dahlonega. Neels Gap is about 14 miles south of Blairsville and three miles south of Vogel State Park. Parking is available 0.3 mile north on the highway.

Maps

For maps, see USGS Neels Gap and Cowrock quadrangles and ATC Chattahoochee National Forest map with this guide.

Shelters, Campsites, and Water

This section has no shelters.
Water is available at Baggs Creek Gap, 1.3 miles south from Tesnatee Gap; at Rock Spring Top, 2.7 miles from Tesnatee Gap; and at Bull Gap, 4.4 miles from Tesnatee Gap. All may be unreliable in dry weather.

Public Accommodations and Supplies

Tesnatee Gap has no sources of supplies or public transportation.
In Neels Gap, the Walasi-Yi Center has a store with hiking and camping supplies. The hostel will resume services in 1999. Write Manager, Walasi-Yi Center, 9710 Gainesville Highway, Blairsville, GA 30512, or call (706) 745-6095. Blood Mountain cabins and store are located about 0.3 mile south on U.S. 19/129, and Goose Creek Cabins are located 3.5 miles north of Neels Gap; free shuttles, (706) 745-5111.

Trail Description, North to South

Miles   **Data**

0.0   Climb steadily from Tesnatee Gap (3,138 feet), around south side of ridge.

0.4   Enter unnamed small gap. Begin long ascent of Cowrock Mountain.

0.8   Reach open, rocky area with excellent views. Turn sharply right, and ascend briefly to the summit of Cowrock Mountain (3,842 feet). Continue on level trail, then descend.

1.3   Cross Baggs Creek Gap (3,591 feet). Spring is down old overgrown road to right. Continue along flat ridgetop. Ascend.

2.1   Reach Wolf Laurel Top (3,766 feet). To left of Trail is open rock face with excellent views. Descend.

2.2   Pass Corbin Horse Stamp. Continue along ridge, passing to right of small knob, ascending and descending slightly.

2.7   Pass to right of Rock Spring Top (3,526 feet), with spring to right of Trail. Swing to the right of ridge, then to right of Turkeypen Mountain (3,550 feet).

3.4   Reach Swaim Gap (3,450 feet). Ascend rocky slope of Levelland Mountain by switchbacks.

3.8   Cross open, rocky area with excellent views on either side of Trail in fall and winter.

4.0   Reach high point of Levelland Mountain (3,942 feet). Descend.

4.4   Reach Bull Gap (3,644 feet). Blue-blazed trail to right leads downhill about 200 yards to spring. Continue gradual descent around northern side of Burnt Ridge.

5.5   Pass through breezeway of Walasi-Yi Center in Neels Gap (3,125 feet) on U.S. 19/129. The old inn now houses a store with hiker supplies, equipment, and food. A hostel will resume services in 1999. To continue on Trail, cross highway.

Trail Description, South to North

Miles

Data

0.0   From U.S. 19/129 in Neels Gap (3,125 feet), go through archway of Walasi-Yi Center. The old inn now houses a store with hiker supplies, equipment, and food. Showers and bunkroom facilities are open, mainly for thru-hikers. A hostel will resume services in 1999. Continue on graded Trail, climbing gradually.

1.1   Reach Bull Gap (3,644 feet). Blue-blazed trail to left leads about 200 yards downhill to spring.

1.5   Reach wooded summit of Levelland Mountain (3,942 feet). Descend slightly.

1.7   Cross rocky, open area with excellent views in fall and winter. Descend on rocky trail.

2.1   Reach Swaim Gap (3,450 feet). Ascend slightly, passing to left of Turkeypen Mountain (3,550 feet), then to left of ridgecrest.

2.8   Pass to left of Rock Spring Top (3,526 feet), with spring to left of Trail. Continue on ridge, ascending and descending slightly.

3.3   Reach Corbin Horse Stamp. Ascend.

3.4   Reach Wolf Laurel Top (3,766 feet). To right of Trail is open, rocky face with excellent views toward Wildcat Ridge. Descend, and continue along ridge.

4.2   In about 20 yards, reach Baggs Creek Gap (3,591 feet). Spring is located down blue-blazed trail on left. Ascend.

4.7   Reach the summit of Cowrock Mountain (3,842 feet). To right of Trail are good views to southeast. Descend slightly to open, rocky area, turn sharply left, and descend steadily.

5.1   Enter small gap. Bear right around knoll, and descend.

5.5   Reach Tesnatee Gap (3,138 feet) and the Richard B. Russell Scenic Highway (Ga. 348). To continue on Trail, cross parking area, and enter woods.

Neels Gap (U.S. 19/129) to Woody Gap (Ga. 60)
Section Fifteen
10.7 Miles

Brief Description of Section

This section of the A.T. is a pleasant day's hike between two paved highways. Despite two long, steep climbs (north to south), the section is a moderately strenuous hike. From Neels Gap (3,125 feet), the Trail ascends gradually, then more steeply by switchbacks, and then gradually through rock outcroppings to the top of Blood Mountain (4,461 feet), which has spectacular views. This two-mile section is perhaps the most hiked section of the Georgia A.T.

The Trail then descends to Slaughter Gap (3,800 feet). Beyond, through short climbs and descents, it gradually loses elevation until the ascent of Big Cedar Mountain (3,737 feet) and the descent to Woody Gap (3,150 feet).

Most of the Trail between Neels Gap and Woody Gap is included in a congressionally designated wilderness area.

Points of Interest

The outstanding features of this section are Blood and Big Cedar mountains. According to Indian legend, a battle fought on Blood Mountain between the Cherokees and the Creeks was so fierce that the mountain "ran red with blood." Lichenous plants covering its rocky slopes sometimes have a reddish hue.

The views from Blood Mountain are spectacular. The rock outcrop near the stone shelter on the summit allows splendid views south. The A.T. is to the right, on the broad, flat ridge leading back to Springer Mountain. Just below the summit, a rock face provides a spectacular panoramic vista. To the southeast is Yonah Mountain, with an unusual, steep rock face. To the northeast, across Neels Gap, is Levelland Mountain. Also to the northeast is the crest of the Blue Ridge with Tray Mountain in the distance.

A two-room stone shelter is located near the summit of Blood Mountain. It was built in the 1930s by the Civilian Conservation Corps and is listed on the National Register of Historic Places. In 1994, at GATC's suggestion, the Forest Service banned all campfires within 300 feet of the Trail in the 3.3-mile section between Slaughter Creek and Neels Gap. The ban, which remains in place, is an effort to allow overused areas to return to their natural state. Fires are prohibited at the shelter as well; the fireplace at the shelter was closed in with stone in 1996. Blood Mountain is the most-visited spot on the A.T. south of Clingmans Dome, and the impact of more than 40,000 visitors a year has taken its toll.

The top of Blood Mountain has no firewood or water. The nearest water sources are near Flatrock Gap, 1.4 miles north, and at Slaughter Creek, 0.9 mile south, but they are unreliable. Fires are prohibited between Neels Gap and Slaughter Creek.

Big Cedar Mountain, one mile north on the Trail from Woody Gap, has excellent views to the south from its rock outcropping.

The Lake Winfield Scott Recreation Area can be reached by a 2.7-mile blue-blazed trail from Slaughter Gap and a one-mile side trail from Jarrard Gap. This area may be closed in winter but, in season, has swimming, a lake, restrooms, picnic areas, and water. Lake Winfield Scott is located on Ga. 180, about 22 miles north of Dahlonega *via* Ga. 60.

Road Approaches

Neels Gap, the northern end of the section, is located on U.S. 19/129, 19 miles north of Cleveland and 22 miles north of Dahlonega. Neels Gap is about 14 miles south of Blairsville and three miles south of Vogel State Park. Parking is available 0.3 mile north on highway.

Woody Gap, at the southern end of the section, is on Ga. 60, about 5.6 miles north of Stone Pile Gap, the junction of Ga. 60 and U.S. 19, and 15 miles north of Dahlonega. The small town of Suches is 1.6 miles north of Woody Gap. Parking is available in the gap; $2.00 parking fee required (1998).

Maps

USGS Neels Gap quadrangle, ATC Chattahoochee National Forest map.

Shelters, Campsites, and Water

This section has two shelters for overnight use. The new (1998) Woods Hole Shelter is located 0.5 mile off the Trail near Bird Gap, 4.0 miles south of Neels Gap. A small stream is nearby. Blood Mountain Shelter is located 2.4 miles from the northern end of the section. This shelter may be closed in the near future, so check with the Forest Service or ATC before planning an overnight stay there. On the northern 3.7 miles of the section, campfires, fire rings, and the gathering of firewood are prohibited.

This section has several water sources: at Flatrock Gap; Slaughter Creek; just south of Jarrard Gap; between Henry and Dan gaps; near Big Cedar Mountain; and in Woody Gap, about 150 yards away on a woods road. There are several stream crossings.

Due to the unreliability of those sources, hikers are advised to obtain water at Neels Gap or Woody Gap.

Public Accommodations and Supplies

Neels Gap, at the northern end of the section, has a store at the Walasi-Yi Center with hiking and camping supplies, showers, and a laundromat. (The hostel will resume services in 1999.) Write Manager, Walasi-Yi Center, 9710 Gainesville Highway, Blairsville, GA 30512, or call (706) 745-6095. Blood Mountain Cabins and store are located about 0.3 mile south on U.S. 19/129, and Goose Creek Cabins are located 3.5 miles north of Neels Gap.

From Woody Gap, it is two miles north to Suches and the intersection of Ga. 60 and Ga. 180, where there is a grocery store and post office. Facilities at Lake Winfield Scott, 2.7 miles from Slaughter Gap, are seasonal and limited. Write USFS, Brasstown Ranger District, Blairsville, GA 30512; call (800) 864-7275.

Cabins, tentsites, showers, laundry service, and a supply concession are located at Vogel State Park (fee charged), about three miles north of Neels Gap off U.S. 19/129. For information, write: Superintendent, Vogel State Park, Blairsville, GA 30512.

No bus lines operate through Neels Gap or Woody Gap. The nearest taxi service to Neels Gap is at Blairsville, 14 miles north; shuttle services are available here and elsewhere on the A.T. Call ATC at (304) 535-6331 for an up-to-date list.

Parking for hikers at Neels Gap is available at the Byron Reece Memorial, 0.3 mile north on the highway. A blue-blazed trail leads from parking area to A.T. on Blood Mountain.

Trail Description, North to South

Miles   **Data**

0.0   On the western side of U.S. 19/129 in Neels Gap (3,125 feet), ascend on graded trail.

0.9   Reach balanced rock on left. In about 100 yards, reach blue-blazed trail on right that leads about one mile to the Byron Reece Memorial, where parking for hikers is available. Water can be found about 0.2 mile down this trail. On A.T. just beyond is the blue-blazed Freeman Trail, to the left, which leads 1.8 miles around the southern slope of Blood Mountain and rejoins the A.T. at Bird Gap.

1.0   Reach Flatrock Gap (3,452 feet). Continue on A.T., ascending by switchbacks.

1.8   Reach rock outcrop with fine views. Bear around to right.

2.3   Reach exposed rock with panoramic vistas. (See "Brief Description of Section.") Climb steeply up rock face.

2.4   Reach open, rocky summit of Blood Mountain (4,461 feet). This is the highest point on the Georgia A.T. and offers splendid views. Summit has no water. Near the summit is the **Blood Mountain Shelter**, a two-room stone building built in the 1930s by the Civilian Conservation Corps (may be closed; check with the Forest Service or ATC). The fireplace has been bricked in, and fires are prohibited in the shelter. Descend steeply.

2.5   Take sharp left, avoiding rocky old road. Begin descent of southwestern side of Blood Mountain by switchbacks.

3.3   Reach Slaughter Gap, where several trails converge. Straight ahead, blue-blazed Slaughter Gap Trail leads about 2.7 miles to Lake Winfield Scott, with **campground** and **parking**. Blue blazes to sharp right lead downhill to water (unreliable). Blue-blazed trail on right through **camping area** is the Duncan Ridge Trail (DRT), a USFS national recreation trail constructed in the 1970s by GATC and USFS. The Duncan Ridge Trail intersects the A.T. at two points, here and one mile north of Three Forks, providing a 65-mile "loop trail" with the A.T. Several hundred yards down the Duncan Ridge Trail is the intersection of the yellow-blazed Coosa Bald Trail, which leads downhill to the right to Vogel State Park, a fee facility. Turn sharply left to continue on A.T., and swing around western slope of Blood Mountain.

3.7 Cross stream. Within 200 feet, cross second stream. Both form headwaters of Slaughter Creek.

4.0 Reach Bird Gap (3,650 feet). Here, blue-blazed Freeman Trail to left leads 1.8 miles around the southern side of Blood Mountain to rejoin the A.T. at Flatrock Gap. In about 60 yards reach blue-blazed trail on right leading about 0.5 mile to **Woods Hole Shelter**. Water available at small stream about halfway along trail (may be dry in dry weather).

4.3 Reach shoulder of Turkey Stamp Mountain (3,770 feet). Descend gradually to wide, flat area. Continue descent. Cross Horsebone Gap (3,450 feet). Ascend.

5.0 Reach shoulder of Gaddis Mountain, and descend around west slope.

5.4 Reach dirt road in Jarrard Gap (3,250 feet). To right, blue-blazed Jarrard Gap Trail, beginning on old road, leads about one mile to Lake Winfield Scott. Stream crosses this trail in about 0.3 mile. Continue uphill on wide trail.

5.5 Intermittent water on left of Trail.

5.9 Reach ridgecrest, known as Burnett Field Mountain (3,478 feet). Continue on Trail, which soon turns left and descends. Follow Trail on southern side of ridge, ascend, then descend into wide, flat area. Continue just below ridgetop. Reach rocky ledge with views to south. Descend by switchbacks.

7.0 Side trail leads right about 200 feet to Henry Gap (3,100 feet). Unpaved road from Henry Gap leads about 0.5 mile to Ga. 180 near Mt. Zion Church. Continue along left side of ridge (Baker Mountain). Descend.

7.8   Reach stream. Bear left, and ascend generally along small ridge.

8.1   Cross Dockery Lake Trail, which leads left about three miles down to Dockery Lake recreation area (no facilities).

8.5   Begin ascent of Granny Top Mountain. At top of ridge in small gap, turn back sharply left, and continue ascent.

8.7   Descend to Dan Gap. Watch for Trail relocation between here and summit of Big Cedar Mountain. Begin ascent of Big Cedar Mountain.

9.2   Pass spring on right of the Trail. Bear right, and continue gradual ascent.

9.7   Reach rocky face of Big Cedar Mountain (3,737 feet), with views to southeast. This rock face is sometimes called "Preaching Rock." Descent is steep.

10.0   Lunsford Gap (3,300 feet) is just to left at top of ridge. Ascend briefly, and continue around right side of ridge.

10.7   Reach picnic area and Ga. 60 in Woody Gap (3,150 feet); parking available. Trail on immediate right leads about 150 yards to spring. To continue on A.T., cross highway. Suches is two miles to the north, with a post office, health clinic, store with laundry facilities, and shower.

Trail Description, South to North

Miles   **Data**

0.0   From Ga. 60 in Woody Gap (3,150 feet), go north through picnic area, and enter woods. Trail to left leads about 150 yards to spring. A.T. climbs gradually along left side of ridge.

0.7   Descend slightly, swinging to left of Lunsford Gap. Beyond, ascent is steep.

1.0   Reach rocky overlook near top of Big Cedar Mountain (3,737 feet), with excellent views to southeast. Continue ascent, then descend gradually.

1.5   Watch for Trail relocation between here and Dan Gap. Bear left, and begin descent.

2.0   Reach Dan Gap, cross old road, and ascend Granny Top Mountain. At bottom of slope on crest, turn back sharply right, and descend.

2.6   Cross Dockery Lake Trail, which leads right about three miles to Dockery Lake recreation area (no facilities). Descend gradually.

2.9   Cross stream. Bear right, follow old road briefly, then ascend, continuing along southern side of Baker Mountain.

3.7   Side trail to left leads about 200 feet to Henry Gap (3,100 feet). Unpaved road from Henry Gap leads about 0.5 mile to Ga. 180 near Mt. Zion Church. Ascend. Reach rock outcrop with view to the south. Descend, and continue just below ridgecrest. Enter flat area on crest. Cross over shoulder of ridge, ascend to ridgecrest, and turn right.

4.8   Pass over flat area known as Burnett Field Mountain (3,478 feet).

5.0   Begin descent.

5.2   Pass intermittent spring in bank to right of Trail.

5.3   Cross dirt road in Jarrard Gap (3,250 feet). Blue-blazed Jarrard Gap Trail to left, beginning on old road, leads about one mile to Lake Winfield Scott. Stream crosses this trail in about 0.3 mile. Ascend, and soon bear left around western side of Gaddis Mountain, just below summit.

5.7   Reach shoulder, and begin descent. Follow ridgecrest, reach Horsebone Gap (3,450 feet), ascend, and pass through flat area. Continue ascent.

6.4   Reach shoulder of Turkey Stamp Mountain (3,770 feet).

6.7   Reach Bird Gap (3,650 feet). Blue-blazed trail on left leads about 0.5 mile to **Woods Hole Shelter**. Water is available at small stream about halfway along Trail (may be dry in dry weather). In about 60 yards, blue-blazed trail to right leads 1.8 miles around southern side of Blood Mountain to Flatrock Gap on the A.T. Ascend gradually, swinging around western side of Blood Mountain.

7.0   Cross stream. Within 200 feet, cross second stream. Both form headwaters of Slaughter Creek. No-campfire zone begins here and ends at Neels Gap.

7.4   Reach Slaughter Gap (3,800 feet). In gap is junction of several trails. Blue-blazed Slaughter Gap Trail to left leads

2.7 miles to Lake Winfield Scott; blue-blazed trail straight ahead leads downhill about 200 feet to unreliable water source. Through **camping area**, bearing left, is a third blue-blazed trail, the Duncan Ridge National Recreation Trail, which leads to Ga. 180 at Wolfpen Gap. The Duncan Ridge Trail (DRT) intersects the A.T. at two points, here and one mile north of Three Forks, providing a 65-mile "loop trail" with the A.T. Several hundred yards down the Duncan Ridge Trail is the intersection of the yellow-blazed Coosa Bald Trail, which leads downhill to the right to Vogel State Park; fee. To continue on A.T., turn sharply right, and ascend southwest side of Blood Mountain.

8.2   Make sharp right turn, and ascend on rocky trail to summit.

8.3   Reach summit of Blood Mountain (4,461 feet). This is the highest point on the Georgia A.T., with views in all directions of the Blue Ridge Mountains. Near the summit is the **Blood Mountain Shelter**, a two-room stone building built in the 1930s by the Civilian Conservation Corps (may be closed; check with the Forest Service or ATC). The fireplace has been bricked in, and fires are prohibited in the shelter. The summit has no water. Cross over open summit area, and descend.

8.4   Reach rock outcropping, with excellent views (see "Brief Description of Section"). Continue steeply down rock face, bear left, then bear right into wooded area.

8.9   Reach rocky overlook, bear around to left. Skirt side of mountain, then descend by switchbacks.

9.7   Reach Flatrock Gap (3,452 feet). In about 50 yards, blue-blazed trail to right leads 1.8 miles around southern slope of Blood Mountain to Bird Gap on the A.T. Just beyond is another blue-blazed trail to the left that leads about one mile to Byron Reece Memorial, where parking for hikers is available. Water can be found 0.2 mile down this trail. Continuing on the A.T., in about 100 yards, reach balanced rock on right, and bear to left side of ridge.

10.7 Reach U.S. 19/129 in Neels Gap (3,125 feet) and end of section.

Woody Gap (Ga. 60) to Hightower Gap
Section Sixteen
11.9 Miles

Brief Description of Section

This is one of the most interesting sections along the Georgia A.T. Here, the Blue Ridge is richly wooded, consisting of long ridges that break gently to the north, more steeply to the south. The Trail follows graded trails and woods roads throughout the section.

North to south, the Trail skirts Black Mountain on a contour and continues with relatively minor elevation change to Gooch Gap and USFS 42 (the Cooper Gap-Suches Road). Beyond Gooch Gap, the Trail follows the crest of Horseshoe Ridge, then follows abandoned logging roads through a deep valley known as Devil's Kitchen (2,500 feet). It then climbs Justus Mountain (3,224 feet) and descends to Cooper Gap and USFS 42. Beyond, the A.T. follows ridgecrests through the Blue Ridge Wildlife Management Area to Hightower Gap (2,854 feet).

Points of Interest

Although not on the A.T., the outstanding peak in this section is Black Mountain (3,742 feet), near Woody Gap. Rock outcrops on several peaks offer fine views to the south.

Road Approaches

The northern end of this section is on Ga. 60 at Woody Gap, about 5.6 miles north of Stone Pile Gap, the junction of Ga. 60 and U.S. 19, and 15 miles north of Dahlonega (on U.S. 19/Ga. 60).

The southern end, Hightower Gap, is located on USFS 42. This road is an unpaved, all-weather road that extends from Ga. 60 at Suches (1.6 miles north of Woody Gap) some 30 miles west to the Doublehead Gap Road east of Ellijay. The Trail crosses USFS 42 in four locations: Gooch Gap, Cooper Gap, Hightower Gap, and near Springer Mountain. The distance from Suches to Hightower Gap is

11.9 miles; to Cooper Gap, 8.8 miles; and to Gooch Gap, 2.7 miles; limited parking is available in the gaps.

At the junction of USFS 42 and 80 in Cooper Gap (Hightower Gap-to-Suches direction), a right turn onto USFS 80 leads about 2.7 miles to a paved highway and a U.S. Army Ranger training installation. A left turn onto paved road leads about nine miles to U.S. 19 just north of Dahlonega.

Maps

USGS Noontootla and Suches quadrangles, and ATC Chattahoochee National Forest map.

Shelters, Campsites, and Water

This section has one shelter, the Gooch Gap Shelter, located just off the Trail on a blue-blazed side trail about 3.6 miles from Woody Gap and 0.3 mile from Gooch Gap (north to south). A spring is approximately 0.2 mile south of the shelter, directly on the Trail. A second spring is located about 100 yards before Gooch Gap (north to south), off the Trail on a blue-blazed trail. Between Gooch Gap and Cooper Gap are several streams.

Public Accommodations and Supplies

No public accommodations are available at either end of this section. At the junction of Ga. 60 and Ga. 180 (about two miles north of Woody Gap on Ga. 60) in Suches is a store with a limited selection of supplies. Next to the store on Ga. 60 is the Suches post office.

No public transportation operates through Woody Gap.

Precautions

November and December are deer-hunting months in the Blue Ridge Wildlife Management Area. Hikers should exercise caution and wear blaze orange.

The Army Rangers use much of the Chattahoochee National Forest for training maneuvers. Hikers might occasionally see or hear evidence of such maneuvers. Army Rangers are under orders not to interfere with hikers.

Trail Description, North to South

Miles   **Data**

0.0   Cross highway (Ga. 60) at Woody Gap (3,150 feet), passing through picnic area on western side of highway; parking available; $2.00 parking fee required (1998). Follow graded trail along steep, heavily wooded southern side of Black Mountain.

1.0   Enter Tritt Gap (3,050 feet). Continue just below ridgecrest. Ascend.

1.4   Reach crest of Ramrock Mountain (3,200 feet), with views to the south. Descend by switchbacks.

1.5   Reach Jacks Gap (3,000 feet). Begin long ascent. Reach top with views to south. Descend gradually, then more steeply.

2.1   Watch for Trail relocation between here and mile 3.0. Pass Liss Gap (2,952 feet), overgrown with poplars. Bear right around northern side of ridge.

2.6   Cross abandoned, eroded road. Ascend, bear left, and cross to left side of ridge.

3.0   Reach ridgetop, and begin gradual descent to Gooch Gap. About 100 yards before Gooch Gap is blue-blazed trail on left that leads about 200 yards to spring.

3.6   Reach unpaved forest road (USFS 42) in Gooch Gap (2,784 feet). To right, road leads about 2.7 miles to Suches, with supplies and a post office (left about 0.4 mile on Ga. 60). To left, road leads 6.1 miles to Cooper Gap and beyond. Cross road, and, in a few yards, reach blue-blazed loop trail that leads straight ahead to **Gooch Gap Shelter** (built by USFS in 1959). Side trail rejoins A.T. in about 0.3 mile. On Trail, bear right through open area.

3.9   Pass blue-blazed loop trail from the **Gooch Gap Shelter**. Spring directly on Trail here. Ascend, and swing around right side of the mountain.

4.6   Reach shallow gap (2,950 feet). Ascend slightly, and follow ridgetop.

5.0   Reach high point of Horseshoe Ridge. Bear right, descending. Leave ridgetop, and follow stream downhill.

5.4   Cross stream. Bear left at bottom of hill, and continue above old pastureland on right.

5.7   Cross Blackwell Creek on footbridge. Continue uphill through rhododendron.

6.2   Cross small stream.

6.4   Cross Justus Creek on footbridge.

6.5   Cross old logging road. To left on this road, it is about 0.5 mile to USFS 42. Begin ascent of Justus Mountain.

7.2   Cross over Phyllis Spur (3,081 feet), and descend.

7.5   Reach saddle (2,900 feet). Beyond, ascent is steep.

7.8   Reach summit of Justus Mountain (3,224 feet). Bear left along ridge, and begin descent by switchbacks. Viewpoint on left of Trail below summit.

8.4   Reach junction of forest roads in Cooper Gap (2,828 feet). Road downhill to left is Cooper Gap Road, USFS 80, which leads 2.7 miles to Army Ranger camp and 14 miles to Dahlonega. Road to sharp left, USFS 42, leads through Gooch Gap to Suches. Road ahead, also USFS 42, leads to Hightower Gap and beyond. Road to immediate right, USFS 15, leads to the Gaddistown settlement. Cross USFS 42, and begin climb.

9.0   Reach summit of Sassafras Mountain (3,336 feet). Continue along ridgetop, then descend.

10.0   Follow Trail through Horse Gap (2,673 feet). USFS 42 is visible to right. Climb to ridgetop. Follow along or near ridgecrest, which generally parallels USFS 42. Good views to south in winter.

11.7   Begin descent to Hightower Gap.

11.9   Reach road junction in Hightower Gap (2,854 feet). USFS 42 to immediate right leads back to Cooper Gap; straight ahead, it leads to Winding Stair Gap and beyond. USFS 69, between those two, leads about two miles to Rock Creek Lake, then to Ga. 60, about 15 miles.

Trail Description, South to North

Miles   **Data**

0.0   From Hightower Gap (2,854 feet), cross USFS 42. (To immediate left, USFS 42 leads to Cooper Gap; behind to right, it leads to Winding Stair Gap; USFS 69, behind to left, leads about two miles to Rock Creek Lake.) Enter woods, and ascend. Follow ridgeline, which generally parallels USFS 42.

1.9   Reach Horse Gap (2,673 feet). USFS 42 is visible to left. Cross gap, and ascend.

2.9   Reach summit of Sassafras Mountain (3,336 feet), and descend.

3.5   Reach forest-road junction in Cooper Gap (2,828 feet). To immediate left, USFS 42 leads back to Hightower Gap; USFS 80, downhill to right, leads 14 miles to Dahlonega. Ahead, USFS 42 leads through Gooch Gap to Suches, about 8.8 miles. Road to far left, USFS 15, leads to Gaddistown settlement. Cross USFS 42, and enter woods to left of road. Begin ascent of Justus Mountain by switchbacks.

4.1   Reach top of Justus Mountain (3,224 feet). Continue on ridge. Descend to saddle.

4.4   Cross saddle (2,900 feet), and continue over Phyllis Spur (3,081 feet). Descend.

5.4   Reach old logging road. To right on this road, it is about 0.5 mile to USFS 42. Cross logging road onto another old road.

5.5   Cross Justus Creek on footbridge (built by GATC), and bear right.

5.9   Cross small stream. Climb slightly to top of small ridge. Descend.

6.2   Cross Blackwell Creek on footbridge (built by GATC). Continue above old pastureland on left.

6.5   Bear right, and cross small stream, then ascend with stream on right.

6.7   Reach crest of Horseshoe Ridge, and bear right, ascending.

6.9   Reach peak of ridge (3,004 feet). Follow ridgecrest.

7.3   Reach shallow gap (2,950 feet). Bear left around northern side of Gooch Mountain.

7.8   Bear left, and descend.

8.0   Reach spring directly on Trail and blue-blazed loop trail to **Gooch Gap Shelter** (up log steps) that rejoins A.T. in about 0.3 mile.

8.3   Pass blue-blazed loop trail from the **Gooch Gap Shelter,** and, in a few yards, enter Gooch Gap (2,784 feet). To left, USFS 42 leads 2.7 miles to Suches, which has supplies and a post office (left 0.4 mile on Ga. 60). To right, it is 6.1 miles back to Cooper Gap. Cross road, and enter wooded area. To right of Trail, about 200 yards down a blue-blazed trail, is a spring. Continue along gradually ascending ridge.

8.9   Watch for Trail relocation between here and mile 9.8. Bear to right of crest, soon turn left, and descend around northern side of ridge.

9.3   Cross abandoned, eroded road. Climb gradually back to ridgecrest.

9.8   Reach Liss Gap (2,952 feet), with stand of large poplar trees. Ascend along ridge. Reach top with views to the south. Descend.

10.4   Reach Jacks Gap (3,000 feet).

10.5   Reach top of Ramrock Mountain (3,200 feet), with views to south. Descent is steep. Continue just below ridgecrest. Ascend.

10.9   Reach Tritt Gap (3,050 feet). Continue on Trail around southern side of Black Mountain.

11.9   Reach Ga. 60 in Woody Gap (3,150 feet).

Hightower Gap to Springer Mountain
Section Seventeen
8.1 Miles

Brief Description of Section

The Appalachian Trail begins, or ends, depending upon one's point of view, at Springer Mountain. Prior to 1958, the terminus was Mt. Oglethorpe, but commercial development necessitated the relocation to a site within the Chattahoochee National Forest.

This section is within the Blue Ridge Wildlife Management Area, where hikers should exercise caution and wear blaze orange during deer-hunting season (November to December). Army Rangers use this section, as well as much of the rest of the Chattahoochee National Forest, for training maneuvers. Hikers may sometimes see or hear evidence of those maneuvers.

From north to south, beginning at Hightower Gap (2,854 feet), the Trail ascends Hawk Mountain but does not cross its summit. From there, it follows ridgecrests, descending alongside Long Creek to Three Forks, where three mountain streams converge to form Noontootla Creek. From Three Forks, the Trail follows an abandoned road along Stover Creek through a magnificent stand of what are believed to be the only virgin hemlocks between Georgia and the Great Smoky Mountains National Park.

From the hemlocks, the Trail leaves the old logging road and crosses Stover Creek, then ascends to the summit of Springer Mountain, the southern terminus of the 14-state footpath.

Points of Interest

Outstanding features of this section are Springer Mountain, the southern terminus of the A.T.; the stand of hemlocks along Stover Creek; the rushing mountain streams that converge in the area called Three Forks; and Long Creek Falls, just off the Trail about 0.9 mile north of Three Forks. In addition, this section has profuse mountain laurel and rhododendron, which bloom in June and July.

Embedded in rock on the summit of Springer Mountain is a bronze plaque of a hiker, with pack on his back, ascending a mountain. This plaque was made by a member of the GATC in 1933, using another GATC member as a model. It was installed on Springer Mountain in 1959 by GATC after the A.T. terminus was moved from Mt. Oglethorpe. Two other plaques, which were installed in the early days of the GATC, are at Neels Gap and Unicoi Gap. The rock overlook on Springer Mountain allows a panoramic view of the Blue Ridge as it crosses Rich Mountain into the Cohutta Mountains to the northwest.

Road Approaches

The northern end of this section is Hightower Gap, at the junction of USFS 42 and USFS 69. USFS 42 is an all-weather road that can be reached from Dahlonega *via* the Cooper Gap Road (USFS 80). Drive north on U.S. 19/Ga. 60 about two miles from Dahlonega to a sign that reads, "Camp Frank D. Merrill." Turn left on paved road, which ends at about the cumulative 10.4-mile point at the Ranger camp. Turn sharply right uphill on graveled road (USFS 80) to Cooper Gap, at about 14.8 miles. In Cooper Gap, turn sharply left onto USFS 42, and continue to Hightower Gap, at 17.0 miles. (**Caution:** Those forest roads are generally passable, except sometimes in winter, but can be very rough in places.)

A longer all-weather route is *via* Woody Gap and Suches. Drive north from Dahlonega on U.S. 19 to junction with Ga. 60 at Stone Pile Gap, approximately 9.4 miles. Here, bear left on Ga. 60, cross mountain and A.T. in Woody Gap, and descend to Suches at 16.6-mile point. Turn left at former store on USFS 42, pass Gooch Gap, and cross the A.T. at 19.4 miles. Reach Cooper Gap and another crossing of the A.T. at 25.5 miles. Continue straight through gap to Hightower Gap, at 29.3 total miles from Dahlonega.

The southern end of the section, the summit of Springer Mountain, may be reached *via* two approaches from the south and one from the north. For directions, see "Approaches to the Southern Terminus of the Appalachian Trail," which follows this section. Limited parking is available at both ends.

Maps

USGS Noontootla quadrangle and ATC Chattahoochee National Forest map.

Shelters, Campsites, and Water

This section has three shelters. Hawk Mountain Shelter is located on the side of Hawk Mountain, about 0.5 mile south of Hightower Gap. The second is the Stover Creek Shelter, about 5.6 miles south of Hightower Gap and 2.5 miles north of Springer Mountain. The third is the Springer Mountain Shelter, located on the summit of Springer Mountain, about 250 yards down a blue-blazed and signed side trail. All three shelters have water sources nearby, but water on Springer Mountain might be scarce in times of drought.

Campsites along this section are available near the shelter on Springer Mountain.

Public Accommodations

The northern end of this section, Hightower Gap, is located at the junction of USFS 42 and 69. It is well within the Chattahoochee National Forest and has no public facilities. Springer Mountain, the southern end of the section and of the A.T., is accessible only by foot.

Trail Description, North to South

Miles	Data

0.0   Leave USFS 42 in Hightower Gap (2,854 feet) at junction with USFS 69. Enter forest, and ascend on graded trail. (USFS 42 leads back to Cooper Gap, Gooch Gap, and Suches; to left, road leads to Winding Stair Gap. USFS 69, on immediate right, leads to Rock Creek and then to Ga. 60, about 15 miles.)

0.5 Reach side trail leading about 0.2 mile to **Hawk Mountain Shelter.** Water is about 400 yards behind shelter. On Trail, water is down slope from flat area, or 0.1 mile south.

0.6 Stream crosses Trail. Continue on Trail along northern side of Hawk Mountain.

1.2 Reach and follow ridgecrest. (Watch for Trail relocation in this area.) Descend.

2.3 Reach gravel logging road. To left is Hickory Flats Cemetery Road, which leads back to USFS 58 near Three Forks. (Down this road about 25 yards, at left turn in gravel road, turn right along dirt road for about 50 yards to reach cemetery. Pavilion and picnic tables at cemetery may be used by hikers.) Cross road, and continue descent on graded trail.

2.6 At bottom of descent, Trail turns left onto old logging road.

3.0 The Benton MacKaye Trail (BMT), marked with white diamond blazes, and the Duncan Ridge Trail (DRT), marked with blue blazes, enter from the right. For the next mile, the three trails share the same route.

3.1 Reach blue-blazed trail to right leading to Long Creek Falls, a spectacular waterfall. Continue on Trail, which parallels Long Creek.

4.0 Reach USFS 58 and area called Three Forks, the convergence of three mountain streams to form Noontootla River. To left, USFS 58 leads 2.6 miles to Winding Stair Gap and USFS 42, which heads left to Hightower Gap. Cross road, and, in a few yards, cross Chester Creek. *Note:* The Duncan Ridge Trail ends at Three Forks; the Benton MacKaye Trail continues along with the A.T. a few hundred yards and turns left up Rich Mountain, recrossing A.T. in about 2.3 miles.

4.5 Cross Stover Creek, and turn left on Trail, which follows abandoned logging road and parallels Stover Creek. For next mile, observe the hemlocks, which may be a virgin stand.

5.5 Turn left off logging road, and descend briefly, crossing stream. Ascend log steps.

5.6 Reach old logging road; **Stover Creek Shelter** is approximately 200 feet to right. Turn left on logging road for about

25 feet, then climb series of log steps on right, and reach another old road. Turn left on this road for about 0.2 mile. Turn right up third set of steps, and ascend around northern slope of Rich Mountain.

6.0   Cross small stream.

6.3   Reach ridgetop, cross Benton MacKaye Trail, and descend gradually.

6.6   Cross small tributary, and, in a few yards, cross Davis Creek. Ascend.

6.9   Cross Benton MacKaye Trail again.

7.2   Reach parking area at USFS 42. Bear around upper (east and then northern) side of parking area, and follow gravel ramp onto USFS 42. To left, road leads 2.6 miles to Winding Stair Gap and continues to Hightower Gap. To right, road leads about 7 miles to Doublehead Gap Road and then to Ellijay. Cross road, and begin ascent of Springer Mountain.

7.9   Come to junction of A.T. with Benton MacKaye Trail. Approximately 20 yards farther is blue-blazed side trail to left leading to **Springer Mountain Shelter** (built in 1993) and spring. Water may be scarce during dry weather. Midway along shelter trail, side trail to right leads about 100 yards to large, open area with **campsites**. (Camping is prohibited on the summit.) Side trail opposite campsite leads to water and shelter.

8.1   Reach summit of Springer Mountain (3,782 feet) and junction of A.T. with blue-blazed Approach Trail from Amicalola Falls State Park. The rock overlook provides an excellent view of the Blue Ridge range as it crosses Rich Mountain and heads to the Cohuttas in northwest Georgia. In the rock at the overlook is a bronze plaque of a hiker, with pack on his back, climbing a mountain. This was installed by the GATC in 1959. On the edge of the rock overlook (above Trail register embedded in rock) is a plaque installed in 1993 by USFS identifying Springer Mountain as the southern terminus of the A.T.

Trail Description, South to North

Miles   **Data**

0.0   The northbound A.T. begins at the summit of Springer
        Mountain (3,782 feet), at the junction with the blue-blazed
        Approach Trail from Amicalola Falls State Park. To the left
        at the summit is overlook with excellent views of the
        western range of the Blue Ridge as it crosses Rich Moun-
        tain and heads to the Cohuttas to northwest. Embedded in
        rock is a bronze plaque, approximately 14 inches by 16
        inches, depicting a hiker with pack on his back, climbing
        a mountain. This plaque was made by a member of the
        GATC in 1933 and installed here in 1959. On the edge of
        rock overlook (above Trail register embedded in rock) is a
        plaque installed in 1993 by USFS noting Springer Moun-
        tain as the southern terminus of the A.T. Because of
        overuse and resource damage, camping is prohibited on
        the summit area. Continue on the Trail along northern
        slope of mountain, descending gradually.

0.2   Reach blue-blazed trail on right to **Springer Mountain
        Shelter** (built in 1993), with water available. Water might
        be scarce in dry weather. Midway along shelter trail, side
        trail to right leads about 100 yards to open area with
        campsites. Side trail opposite campsite leads to water and
        shelter. On A.T., about 20 yards beyond shelter trail, reach
        junction of A.T. with Benton MacKaye Trail (marked with
        off-white diamond blazes).

0.9   Reach USFS 42; to right, road leads 2.6 miles back to
        Winding Stair Gap and continues to Hightower Gap; to
        left, road leads about seven miles to Doublehead Gap and
        to Ellijay. To continue on A.T., cross road, and climb steps
        to gravel parking area. Bear left, passing information
        board, and bear right above parking area. Enter woods,
        swinging around southern, then eastern, side of knob on
        level trail.

1.2   Cross Benton MacKaye Trail.

1.5   Reach Davis Creek. In a few yards, cross a small tributary.

1.8   Reach ridgecrest where A.T. again crosses Benton MacKaye Trail. Begin descent along northern slope of Rich Mountain.

2.1   Reach stream. Soon, descend several steps, and turn left on old road for about 0.2 mile.

2.5   Descend series of log steps, and reach another old logging road. **Stover Creek Shelter** is located approximately 200 feet to the left on roadbed. Descend additional log steps, cross stream, and ascend slightly.

2.6   Turn sharply right onto old logging road. Within the next mile, ancient hemlocks might be a virgin stand. Continue on Trail along Stover Creek.

3.6   Make right turn, and cross Stover Creek.

3.9   The BMT rejoins the A.T. and follows the route of the A.T. for approximately one mile. Between Three Forks and the turnoff of the BMT, the Duncan Ridge Trail (DRT) also shares the same route. The DRT is marked with two-by-six-inch blue blazes.

4.0   Cross log bridge over Chester Creek.

4.1   Reach USFS 58 and area called Three Forks, the convergence of three mountain streams to form Noontootla Creek. To right, USFS 58 leads about 2.6 miles back to Winding Stair Gap and junction with USFS 42, which leads left back to Hightower Gap. Cross road, and continue on Trail up abandoned logging road, barricaded to vehicular traffic. This old road parallels Long Creek.

5.0   Reach blue-blazed trail to Long Creek Falls, a spectacular waterfall, to left of the Trail. In about 0.1 mile, the Benton MacKaye Trail and the Duncan Ridge Trail turn left off old road while A.T. continues (Watch for Trail relocation in this area.).

5.5   Cross small stream, and turn right, uphill, off old road through rhododendron thickets. Cross two old logging roads.

5.8   Reach graveled logging road. (Along this road to the right, bear right again off gravel road, and reach Hickory Flats Cemetery. Pavilion and picnic tables located here may be used by hikers.) Cross road, and ascend along ridge, following crest.

6.9 Bear left off ridgecrest, and skirt northern side of Hawk Mountain.

7.5 Cross stream, a water source for shelter ahead; however, stream may be dry during dry months.

7.6 Come to side trail leading about 0.2 mile to **Hawk Mountain Shelter**. Water can be found about 400 yards behind shelter. Continue on Trail, descending gradually.

8.1 Descend into Hightower Gap (2,854 feet) and junction of USFS 42 with USFS 69. (USFS 42 leads ahead to Cooper Gap, Gooch Gap, and Suches; to right, road leads back to Winding Stair Gap. USFS 69, on immediate left, leads to Rock Creek.) To continue on A.T., cross USFS 42, and enter woods.

Approaches to the Southern Terminus of the Appalachian Trail

The southern terminus of the Appalachian Trail is designated by the summit marker on Springer Mountain. Since Springer Mountain is the starting point for hundreds of northbound thru-hikers each spring, and because the summit of Springer Mountain is well within the Chattahoochee National Forest and accessible only by foot travel, detailed directions are given in this chapter for the several most-used approaches to Springer Mountain. Those include: the approach to Springer Mountain *via* Amicalola Falls State Park and the blue-blazed Approach Trail from the park to the summit of Springer Mountain; a road approach to the blue-blazed Approach Trail *via* Nimblewill Gap, where the Approach Trail crosses; and road approaches to Springer Mountain from the north *via* the A.T. For long-distance hikers, the approach to Springer Mountain from Amicalola Falls State Park, although longer and more strenuous, may be preferable because of available parking and other facilities. The other road approaches require travel over long and often rough, unpaved roads.

1. Approach to Springer Mountain *via* Amicalola Falls State Park (8.8 miles)

General Information

Amicalola Falls State Park is located in Dawson County, about 15 miles northwest of Dawsonville. The falls for which the park was named are formed by the plunge of Amicalola Creek in several cascades down the side of Amicalola Mountain, a distance of 729 feet. The falls create a spectacular "silver streak" on the mountainside, visible from several points along the highways in this vicinity. The 406-acre Amicalola Falls State Park was established in 1948 and has a visitors center, a lodge and restaurant, a campground, picnic areas, grills, furnished cabins, showers, and a trail shelter. The Len Foote Hike Inn at Amicalola Falls, a "walk-in" lodge, with meals and lodging, opened in 1998. A 5-mile loop trail to the lodge connects at both ends with the A.T. Approach Trail. For information, contact the state park. Address mail to: Superintendent, Amicalola Falls State Park, 240 Amicalola Falls State Park Road, Dawsonville, GA 30534. A telephone is located at the park entrance. Note: Park gates open at 7 a.m. and close at 10 p.m.

Amicalola Falls State Park is accessible by Gainesville Cab Company, (770) 534-5355, and Lanier Taxi, (770) 297-0066 from Gainesville. Gainesville can be reached from Atlanta's Trailways Bus Depot by American Coach Lines, and shuttle service is available from Dahlonega (no bus service to Dahlonega from Atlanta). One shuttle service in operation at time of publication was Appalachian Adventures, located in Gainesville. Since Trail guides are updated at four- or five-year intervals, hikers are advised to write the Georgia A.T. Club, P.O. Box 654, Atlanta, Ga. 30301, or consult the *Appalachian Trail Thru-hikers' Companion,* published annually by ATC, for the latest services and prices. And, you may call ATC at (304) 535-6331 for an up-to-date list of shuttles. Arrangements should be made well in advance. It is about 19 miles from Dahlonega to Amicalola Falls State Park.

Road Approaches to Amicalola Falls State Park

The most common road approaches to Amicalola Falls State Park and Springer Mountain are from, or through, Atlanta, Gainesville, Dahlonega, Dawsonville, or Ellijay. *From Atlanta* go about 38 miles north (from I-285) on Ga. 400/U.S. 19, turn left at stoplight on Ga. 52 for 6.5 miles to Dawsonville. (To Dahlonega, continue on Ga. 400/U.S. 19 about nine additional miles to end of four-lane; turn left on Ga. 60 for five miles to Dahlonega square.) *From the square in Dawsonville,* proceed north on County Road 224. At 2.5 miles, at intersection with Ga. 136; bear left. At 9.4 miles at intersection with Ga. 183, go straight ahead. At 12.2 miles, turn right on Ga. 52. At 13.8 miles, at entrance of state park, turn left. *From the square in Dahlonega,* follow Ga. 52 west for about 19 miles to the entrance of the state park; turn right. *From Gainesville,* go west on Ga. 53 about 22 miles to Dawsonville, or west on Ga. 60 about 25 miles to Dahlonega. *From Ellijay,* go east on Ga. 52 for about 20 miles to state park entrance.

Approach Trail to Springer Mountain from Amicalola Falls State Park

Trail Description, South to North

Miles	Data

0.0   The Approach Trail begins behind the visitors center in the park (1,700 feet). Go through playground, and begin ascent of ridge. Trail **shelter** is about 200 feet to left of Trail. Continue ascent, swinging to right, then bearing left, gradually ascending along side of ridge just below service road. After 0.7 mile, reach gravel service road, and follow road uphill to top of falls.

1.1   Reach gate near top of falls (2,400 feet). (To view falls from above, go beyond gate, turn left, and descend steps to walkway. Parking areas are on far side of falls and also ahead beyond gate.) At gate, bear right off dirt road, and ascend. Cross trail to Amicalola Park Lodge.

1.2   Cross paved road, which leads right to lodge and restaurant. Ascend slightly.

1.3   Yellow-blazed trail to right leads five miles to the Len Foote Hike Inn (reservations required). Descend. Reach flat area with stream on left. Cross small footbridge, bear left, and cross a second footbridge.

1.5   Reach USFS 46 (Nimblewill Gap Road), which leads left to Amicalola Falls Park and right to High Shoals Road (formerly Cemetery Road). Beyond High Shoals Road, USFS 46 might be rough and impassable after a few miles. On Trail, climb steps, and climb steeply around side of ridge. Follow ridgecrest, descend, then ascend.

3.2   Reach High Shoals Road. To left, road leads to old cemetery; to right, road leads 0.3 mile to Amicalola Falls-Frosty Mountain Road, USFS 46. Cross High Shoals Road, and continue ascent. Follow ridgecrest, then skirt western side of ridge.

4.1   Trail begins steep ascent of Frosty Mountain. Reach crest, and continue on level section.

4.8   Reach open, grassy top of Frosty Mountain and site of old fire tower. Overgrown trail to right leads several hundred yards to spring; unreliable in dry weather. Continuation on right of forest road, approaching from left, leads several yards to **campsite**. To continue on Approach Trail, cross clearing, and descend.

5.1   Cross USFS 46 again. Road to right leads four miles to Amicalola Falls and 5.3 miles to Ga. 52; to left, it leads 1.5 miles to Nimblewill Gap. Ascend, and continue along ridge.

5.4   Yellow-blazed trail to right leads one mile to the Len Foote Hike Inn (reservations required) and six miles back to Amicalola Falls.

5.7   Reach Woody Knob (3,400 feet). Bear left, and descend steeply.

6.0   Reach road crossing in Nimblewill Gap (3,100 feet). USFS 28 to right leads 7.4 miles to Nimblewill Church and 10 miles to Ga. 52. USFS 46, down mountain to left, leads to Bucktown Settlement. Road sharply up mountain leads 1.5 miles back to Frosty Mountain. Cross road in Nimblewill Gap, and ascend.

6.2   Reach flat ridge. Begin gradual ascent around left (western) side of Black Mountain. Cross shoulder, and descend gradually. Just beyond shoulder to the left of trail is unreliable spring. Along here, and to left of Trail, Springer Mountain can be seen ahead.

7.3   Reach gap (3,400 feet). **Black Gap Shelter** is located about 300 feet to the left of trail. Water is downhill to the right several hundred yards. Ascend, and follow flat ridge, then turn right to ascend gradually along side of mountain. Turn back sharply left, and continue ascent to summit.

8.8   Reach the A.T. and rock overlook on the summit of Springer Mountain (3,782 feet). At overlook area is a bronze terminus plaque showing hiker facing north, and a Trail register inside rock. Bare, rocky ledges allow excellent views of almost unbroken mountain range. This is an outstanding point in the southern Appalachians. The two forks of the Blue Ridge that separate below Roanoke, Virginia, join here. For an account of the geographical structure of the southern Appalachians, see "The Appalachian Mountain

System," by Arnold Guyot, in *American Journal of Science and Arts*, vol. 31, second series, March 1961, pp. 158-187.

2. Road Approaches to Blue-Blazed Approach Trail *via* Nimblewill Gap (2.8 miles)

This is the nearest road approach to Springer Mountain *via* the blue-blazed Approach Trail from Amicalola Falls State Park. Follow directions from Atlanta and Gainesville on page 171 to Dawsonville or Dahlonega. *From Dawsonville:* Take Ga. 9 north for 10.4 miles, turn left at Ga. 52, and go 4.5 miles to Nimblewill Church Road (a loop road that returns to Ga. 52) at small, closed store. *From Dahlonega:* Follow Ga. 52 west for about nine miles to Nimblewill Church Road. From old store, turn right, go 2.5 miles to Nimblewill Church. Continue straight ahead onto unpaved road (USFS 28-2), while paved road bears left back to Ga. 52. *From Ellijay:* Go east on Ga. 52 about 27 miles (about 6.5 miles beyond Amicalola State Park) to the western end of Nimblewill Church Road. Turn left, and go about two miles to Nimblewill Church, and turn left onto unpaved USFS 28-2. From Nimblewill Church it is about eight miles to Nimblewill Gap and the crossing of the Approach Trail. *Use caution.* This road is very rough and may be impassable by car, especially during bad weather. To right, trail leads 2.8 miles to the summit of Springer Mountain; to left, trail leads six miles back to Amicalola Falls State Park. There is limited parking available in the gap.

3. Road Approach to Springer Mountain *via* USFS 42 (0.9 mile)

The closest approach road to Springer Mountain is USFS 42, a rough, unpaved road that extends from Ga. 60 in Suches some 30 miles to Doublehead Gap Road, crossing the A.T. at Gooch Gap, Cooper Gap, Hightower Gap, and near Springer Mountain. From the parking area on USFS 42 at the foot of Springer Mountain, it is 0.9 mile to the summit south *via* the A.T.

There are three road approaches to Springer Mountain *via* USFS 42. All involve travel over rough, unpaved USFS 42 and/or USFS 77. *From Dahlonega or Dawsonville:* Follow directions to Ga. 52 and

Nimblewill Church Road. *On Nimblewill Church Road:* Go 2.4 miles to unpaved USFS 28-1, just before Nimblewill Church. Turn right, and go approximately two miles, bear left onto USFS 77 for approximately seven miles to USFS 42 in Winding Stair Gap. Turn left and go about 2.5 miles to parking area and crossing of A.T. near Springer Mountain. USFS 42 north from Springer Mountain parking area is usually in somewhat better condition; it may be approached from Ga. 52 southeast of Ellijay or northwest of Amicalola State Park. *From Ellijay:* Go east on Ga. 52 about 5.2 miles, turn left on Big Creek Road. Go 12.8 miles to Mt. Pleasant Church (on left) at Doublehead Gap. Turn right onto unpaved USFS 42 for 6.8 miles to A.T. crossing at Springer parking area. *From Amicalola State Park:* Go north on Ga. 52 about 14 miles to Big Creek Road, and follow directions from Ellijay above. *From Ga. 60 in Suches:* It is about 18 miles *via* USFS 42 to the parking area near Springer Mountain. Across USFS 42 from the parking area, the A.T. leads about 0.9 mile south to the summit of Springer Mountain. (For detailed description of Trail, see Section Seventeen, Hightower Gap to Springer Mountain.)

Loop Hiking in Georgia Using the Appalachian, Benton MacKaye, and Duncan Ridge Trails

In 1978, with the building of a bridge over the Toccoa River, an approximately 35-mile loop trail—under construction by the Georgia Appalachian Trail Club and the Chattahoochee National Forest for more than a decade—was completed and designated "Loop Trail in Georgia." This trail formed a figure-eight with the Appalachian Trail, leaving the A.T. on Springer Mountain, rejoining it later in the Three Forks area, and again at Slaughter Gap, thus providing a challenging hike and bringing the hiker back to the point of origin.

In 1980, prior to assuming full maintenance and management of the A.T. in Georgia, GATC relinquished maintenance of the Loop Trail. The Chattahoochee National Forest designated that portion of the Loop Trail from Three Forks to Slaughter Gap the Duncan Ridge National Recreation Trail (the DRT is marked by two-by-six-inch blue blazes). For more information on the Duncan Ridge Trail, write to the USFS, Chattahoochee National Forest, 1755 Cleveland Highway, Gainesville, GA 30501; telephone, (770) 536-0541.

Also in 1980, the Benton MacKaye Trail Association began the construction of a hiking trail (marked with off-white diamond blazes) that, as originally planned, would start at Springer Mountain and proceed northeast, then west to an area in Georgia east of the Cohuttas. From there, the trail is planned to proceed along the ridgecrest of Tennessee-North Carolina through the Great Smoky Mountains National Park. The Benton MacKaye Trail (BMT) was named for the founder of the A.T. and was planned partly along a route originally planned for the A.T.

As detailed below, the BMT diverges from the A.T. on Springer Mountain and proceeds *via* Big Stamp Gap to cross the A.T. twice in the Rich Mountain vicinity, then joins the A.T. near Three Forks (a second and longer loop hike), before heading northeast to the Toccoa River and the Cohuttas. For detailed information and maps (also available from ATC), write to the Benton MacKaye Trail Association, P.O. Box 53271, Atlanta, GA 30355.

Those two major trails that branch from the A.T. in Georgia are detailed below. Distances noted in the left margin represent the location on the A.T. (south to north from Springer Mountain at 0.0 miles) at which either the BMT or the DRT intersect with the A.T.

The Benton MacKaye Trail

Trail Description, South to North

Miles   **Data**

0.2   On the A.T., approximately 20 yards north of the blue-blazed side trail to the Springer Mountain Shelter (water available), the BMT (marked with white diamond blazes) diverges to the right to descend to USFS 42 at Big Stamp Gap. It follows old logging roads to rejoin the A.T. near the site of the former Cross Trails Shelter at 3.2 miles (**campsites** and water are nearby).

1.2   The BMT crosses the A.T. here and again on Rich Mountain (pay attention to markings) to descend to a third junction with the A.T. near Three Forks, at approximately 5.8 miles from Springer Mountain on the BMT. Thus, taken together, the A.T. and the BMT provide two loop hikes in this scenic area, one of approximately 4.4 miles (Springer Mountain to the Cross Trails site on one trail and return on the other), the other approximately 9.9 miles (Springer Mountain to Three Forks on one trail and return on the other).

4.1   At the area known as Three Forks (where three rushing mountain streams join to form the Noontootla Creek), *three* trails (the A.T., BMT, and DRT) all follow the same treadway for approximately one mile. **Campsites** are numerous and attractive, and water is plentiful.

5.0   Come to blue-blazed side trail to left to Long Creek Falls, a spectacular waterfall. Just beyond, both the BMT and the DRT turn left to leave the A.T., cross Long Creek, and head generally northeast. Both trails cross a grassy area with good views of Springer Mountain to the south; climb the John Dick Mountains; descend to Bryson Gap, with good campsites and water; cross the Toccoa River on a 260-foot suspension bridge (good campsites and water); ascend Toonowee Mountain (2,720 feet); then descend to Ga. 60 (to right, east, is store and supplies). Both trails then cross Ga. 60, cross Little Skeenah Creek, steeply ascend Wallalah Mountain (3,090 feet), Licklog Mountain (3,472 feet), and then Rhodes Mountain (3,380 feet), where the BMT and the DRT diverge. The distance from Springer Mountain to Rhodes Mountain *via* the BMT is approximately 21.5 miles.

From the summit of Rhodes Mountain (not on the A.T.), the BMT turns left, to the west, crosses a paved road at Skeenah Gap, and passes through Payne Gap to reach Wilscot Gap and Ga. 60, approximately 27.3 miles from its origin on Springer Mountain. The BMT then climbs Tipton Mountain (3,147 feet) and Brawley Mountain (3,027 feet) to descend to Garland Gap and Dial Road, at approximately 34.4 miles.

Beyond, the BMT follows roads for several miles and heads generally west to join the Rich Mountain Trail briefly, to climb Scroggin Knob, then to descend to Ga. 5/U.S. 76 at the Cherrylog Church, approximately 44.2 miles from its origin on Springer Mountain. From here, it heads generally west, following a paved road for several miles, and then a scenic ridge to the eastern edge of the Cohutta Wilderness. Here, it heads north and crosses into Tennessee at milepoint 78.6. Construction is continuing into Tennessee.

The Duncan Ridge Trail

Trail Description, South to North

Miles   **Data**

4.1   The southern terminus of the Duncan Ridge Trail (DRT), a national recreation trail, is at Three Forks. For approximately one mile, it shares its treadway with the A.T. and the BMT.

5.0   The DRT reaches a blue-blazed side trail at Long Creek Falls. Beyond, the DRT and the BMT diverge to the left from the A.T. to climb the John Dick Mountains, to descend to Bryson Gap (water), to cross the Toccoa River, to climb Toonowee Mountain (2,720 feet), and finally to descend to Ga. 60 (to right, east, is store and supplies). The DRT and BMT then cross Ga. 60 and Little Skeenah Creek and climb Wallalah, Licklog, and Rhodes mountains. On the summit of Rhodes Mountain, the DRT heads east (straight ahead) while the BMT heads north and west. (The DRT is poorly maintained and may be difficult to follow.) From Rhodes Mountain summit, where the DRT and the BMT diverge, the DRT (marked with two-by-six-inch blue blazes) heads generally east to pass through Fish Gap, skirt Fish Knob, pass Akin Gap, and descend to Mulky Gap (2,770 feet) and USFS 4, which leads north to U.S. 76 and south to the Cooper Gap Scenic Area and Ga. 60. The DRT then climbs Wildcat Knob (3,500 feet) and Buck Knob to descend to Bryant Gap, at approximately 22.4 miles from its origin at Three Forks. The DRT crosses Ga. 180 and climbs the eastern side of Slaughter Mountain, then reaches its northern terminus at another junction with the A.T., at Slaughter Gap.

23.6   From Three Forks, the southern terminus of the DRT (and junction with the A.T.), to Slaughter Gap, its northern terminus (and junction with the A.T.), the distances are approximately 31.7 miles on the DRT and 23.6 miles on the A.T., a challenging loop hike of approximately 55.3 miles. For more information and map, write to the USFS, Chattahoochee National Forest (see page 180).

Important Addresses

Appalachian Trail Conference
P.O. Box 807
Harpers Ferry, WV 25425
(304) 535-6331
<www.atconf.org>

Appalachian Trail Conference
TN/NC/GA Regional Office
P.O. Box 2750
Asheville, NC 28802
(828) 254-3708

Smoky Mountains Hiking Club
P.O. Box 1454
Knoxville, TN 37938

Nantahala Hiking Club
31 Carl Slagle Road
Franklin, NC 28734

Georgia Appalachian Trail Club
P.O. Box 654
Atlanta, GA 30301
(404) 634-6495

National Forests in
North Carolina
P.O. Box 2750
Asheville, NC 28802-2750
(828) 257-4200

Nantahala National Forest
Wayah Ranger District
90 Sloan Road
Franklin, NC 28734
(828) 524-6441

Nantahala National Forest
Cheoah Ranger District
Rt. 1, Box 16-A
Robbinsville, NC 28771
(828) 479-6431

Nantahala National Forest
Tusquitee Ranger District
201 Woodland Drive
Murphy, NC 28906
(828) 837-5152

Great Smoky Mountains
National Park
107 Park Headquarters Road
Gatlinburg, TN 37738
(423) 436-1200

Chattahoochee National Forest
1755 Cleveland Highway
Gainesville, GA 30501
(770) 536-0541

Quad Map Sales

Earth Science
Information Center
Reston ESIC-USGS
507 National Center
Reston, VA 20192
(703) 648-6892
(202) 208-4047

Summary of Distances

Great Smoky Mountains National Park

North to South		South to North
0.0	Davenport Gap, Tenn. 32, N.C. 284	71.0
0.9	**Davenport Gap Shelter** side trail	70.1
5.2	Mt. Cammerer Tower side trail	65.8
8.0	**Cosby Knob Shelter**	63.0
8.6	Cosby Knob	62.4
11.9	Snake Den Ridge Trail	59.1
13.8	Mt. Guyot side trail	57.2
15.7	**Tricorner Knob Shelter** side trail	55.3
16.7	Mt. Chapman	54.3
18.2	Mt. Sequoyah	52.8
20.9	**Pecks Corner Shelter** side trail	50.1
22.2	Bradleys View	48.8
25.5	Porters Gap, The Sawteeth	45.5
27.4	Charlies Bunion	43.6
28.6	Boulevard Trail	42.4
31.3	Newfound Gap, U.S. 441	39.7
33.0	Indian Gap	38.0
35.8	**Mt. Collins Shelter** side trail	35.2
38.0	Mt. Love	33.0
39.2	Clingmans Dome	31.8
42.1	**Double Spring Gap Shelter**	28.9
43.6	Silers Bald	27.4
43.8	**Silers Bald Shelter**	27.2
46.5	Buckeye Gap	24.5
49.1	Sams Gap	21.9
49.3	**Derrick Knob Shelter**	21.7
50.4	Sugar Tree Gap	20.6
52.8	Mineral Gap	18.2
53.8	Thunderhead, eastern summit	17.2

54.4	Rockytop	16.6
55.6	**Spence Field Shelter** on Eagle Creek Trail	15.4
58.1	**Russell Field Shelter**	12.9
59.0	Little Abrams Gap	12.0
60.4	Devils Tater Patch	10.6
60.7	**Mollies Ridge Shelter**	10.3
62.1	Ekaneetlee Gap	8.9
63.5	Doe Knob	7.5
65.8	**Birch Spring Shelter** side trail	5.2
67.0	Shuckstack	4.0
71.0	Little Tennessee River	0.0

Nantahala National Forest and
Chattahoochee National Forest

0.0	Little Tennessee River, north bank; Fontana Dam	163.5
0.7	**Fontana Dam Shelter** side trail	162.8
1.8	N.C. 28	161.7
4.5	Walker Gap	159.0
5.9	Black Gum Gap	157.6
7.3	**Cable Gap Shelter**	156.2
8.2	Yellow Creek Gap	155.3
10.6	Cody Gap	152.9
11.4	Hogback Gap	152.1
13.2	Brown Fork Gap	150.3
13.4	**Brown Fork Gap Shelter** side trail	150.1
14.8	Sweetwater Gap	148.7
15.8	Stecoah Gap	147.7
17.9	Simp Gap	145.6
18.9	Locust Cove Gap	144.6
21.3	Cheoah Bald	142.2
22.5	**Sassafras Gap Shelter** side trail	141.0
23.4	Swim Bald	140.1
26.3	Grassy Gap	137.2
27.8	Wright Gap	135.7
29.4	Nantahala River, U.S. 19, Wesser, N.C.	134.1
30.2	**Rufus Morgan Shelter**	133.3
35.1	Wesser Creek Trail, **Wesser Bald Shelter** side trail	128.4
35.9	Wesser Bald	127.6

37.3	Tellico Gap	126.2
40.2	Copper Ridge Bald	123.3
40.9	**Cold Spring Shelter**	122.6
42.1	Burningtown Gap	121.4
44.4	Licklog Gap	119.1
46.6	Wayah Bald	116.9
48.5	Wine Spring	115.0
50.8	Wayah Gap, N.C. 1310	112.7
52.5	**Siler Bald Shelter** side trail (northern end)	111.0
53.0	**Siler Bald Shelter** side trail (southern end	110.5
54.7	Panther Gap, **campsites**	108.8
55.6	Swinging Lick Gap	107.9
56.7	Winding Stair Gap	106.8
59.8	Wallace Gap, U.S. 64, **Standing Indian Campground**	103.7
60.4	Rock Gap	103.1
60.5	**Rock Gap Shelter** side trail	103.0
63.0	Glassmine Gap	100.5
65.8	**Big Spring Shelter** side trail	97.7
66.4	Albert Mountain	97.1
66.7	Bear Pen Trail, USFS 67	96.8
68.0	Mooney Gap, USFS 83	95.5
68.9	Betty Creek Gap	94.6
72.6	**Carter Gap Shelter** side trail	90.9
73.0	Timber Ridge Trail	90.5
74.0	Coleman Gap	89.5
75.8	Beech Gap	87.7
78.7	Lower Trail Ridge Trail to Standing Indian Mountain Summit	84.8
80.2	**Standing Indian Shelter**	83.3
81.1	Deep Gap, USFS 71	82.4
83.2	Wateroak Gap	80.3
84.1	Chunky Gal Trail	79.4
84.3	Whiteoak Stamp	79.2
85.1	**Muskrat Creek Shelter**	78.4
86.0	Sassafras Gap	77.5
86.5	Courthouse Bald	77.0
87.9	Bly Gap	75.6
88.1	North Carolina-Georgia Line	75.4
89.9	Rich Cove Gap	73.6

91.1	Blue Ridge Gap	72.4
91.7	As Knob	71.8
92.4	**Plumorchard Gap Shelter** side trail	71.1
93.5	Bull Gap	70.0
94.9	Cowart Gap	68.6
96.7	Dicks Creek Gap, U.S. 76	66.8
97.9	Moreland Gap	65.6
98.9	Powell Mountain	64.6
100.2	**Deep Gap Shelter** side trail	63.3
100.9	Kelly Knob	62.6
102.0	Addis Gap	61.5
102.8	Sassafras Gap	60.7
103.9	Blue Ridge Swag	59.6
107.3	**Tray Mountain Shelter** side trail	56.2
107.6	Tray Mountain	55.9
108.4	Tray Gap, Tray Mountain Road, USFS 79	55.1
109.2	"Cheese factory"	54.3
110.1	Indian Grave Gap	53.4
111.5	Rocky Mountain	52.0
112.8	Unicoi Gap, Ga. 75	50.7
114.2	Blue Mountain	49.3
115.0	**Blue Mountain Shelter** side trail	48.5
116.6	Red Clay Gap	46.9
117.2	Chattahoochee Gap	46.3
118.4	Cold Springs Gap	45.1
120.8	Poplar Stamp Gap	42.7
122.2	**Low Gap Shelter**	41.3
122.8	Sheep Rock Top	40.7
123.9	Wide Gap	39.6
124.5	Poor Mountain	39.0
125.5	White Oak Stamp	38.0
126.4	Hogpen Gap, Ga. 348	37.1
126.6	**Whitley Gap Shelter** side trail	36.9
127.3	Tesnatee Gap, Ga. 348	36.2
128.1	Cowrock Mountain	35.4
129.4	Wolf Laurel Top	34.1
129.5	Corbin Horse Stamp	34.0
130.7	Swaim Gap	32.8
131.3	Levelland Mountain	32.2
131.7	Bull Gap	31.8

132.8	Neels Gap, U.S. 19/129, Walasi-Yi-Center	30.7
133.8	Flatrock Gap	29.7
135.2	**Blood Mountain Shelter**	28.3
136.1	Slaughter Gap	27.4
136.8	Bird Gap, **Woods Hole Shelter**	26.7
138.2	Jarrard Gap	25.3
138.7	Burnett Field Mountain	24.8
143.5	Woody Gap, Ga. 60	20.0
144.9	Ramrock Mountain	18.6
147.1	USFS 42, **Gooch Gap Shelter** side trail (north)	16.4
147.4	**Gooch Gap Shelter** side trail (south)	16.1
149.2	Blackwell Creek	14.3
149.9	Justus Creek	13.6
151.3	Justus Mountain	12.2
151.9	Cooper Gap, USFS 42, USFS 80, USFS 15	11.6
152.5	Sassafras Mountain	11.0
153.5	Horse Gap	10.0
155.4	Hightower Gap, USFS 42, USFS 58	8.1
155.9	**Hawk Mountain Shelter** side trail	7.6
158.4	Benton MacKaye and Duncan Ridge Trails	5.1
158.5	Long Creek Falls side trail	5.0
159.4	Three Forks, USFS 58	4.1
159.9	Stover Creek	3.6
161.0	**Stover Creek Shelter** side trail	2.5
162.6	USFS 42	0.9
163.3	**Springer Mountain Shelter** side trail	0.2
163.5	Springer Mountain	0.0

Index